seasons in my garden

"Walking with Elizabeth Wagner through *Seasons in My Garden* is to understand what it means to live a contemplative life. Eliciting wisdom from her encounters with Maine's red apples, peach trees, English roses, and even intractable Japanese beetles, she meditates on nature with the same mindfulness that she uses to consider scripture. In doing so, she provides us with mini-retreats for the soul in each beautifully written chapter."

Judith Valente
Author of *Atchison Blue*

"*Seasons in My Garden* celebrates the earthy heart of Benedictine wisdom in this lovely collection of meditations on gardening, spirituality, and the seasons of the year."

Carl McColman
Author of *Befriending Silence*

"In her lovely book, Sr. Elizabeth Wagner weaves liturgy, prayer, gardening, and praise into a beautiful lectio divina of nature. Her writing leads us into a deeper contemplation of the Creator and his creation."

Margaret Rose Realy
Author of *A Catholic Gardener's Spiritual Almanac*

"In this insightful and engaging book, Sr. Wagner invites us into a spiritual life where one touches God and the true self among bare trees, blooming roses, and a listening heart. Wagner tends her garden and plants seeds in the soil of our souls. A delightful book, filled with wisdom!"

Colette Lafia
Author of *Seeking Surrender*

Meditations from a Hermitage

seasons in my garden

ELIZABETH WAGNER

AVE MARIA PRESS AVE Notre Dame, Indiana

Some of the essays in this book appeared previously: "Blessed Boredom" in *Gryffin* in Fall 2013; "Standing Far Off" in *The Forge* for October 2011, and in *Schuylkill Valley Journal* for Fall 2011; "Abundance" in *Eclectica Magazine* for April 15, 2011; "Goldenrod Days" in *Willow Review*, May 2011; a version of "Bush Hogs and Blueberries" appeared as "Bush Hogs, Blueberries and God" in *GreenPrints* in Spring 2015; and a version of "Japanese Beetles" appeared as "Suscipe" in *GreenPrints* in Summer 2012.

© 2016 by Elizabeth Wagner

All rights reserved. No part of this book may be used or reproduced in any manner whatsoever, except in the case of reprints in the context of reviews, without written permission from Ave Maria Press®, Inc., P.O. Box 428, Notre Dame, IN 46556, 1-800-282-1865.

Founded in 1865, Ave Maria Press is a ministry of the United States Province of Holy Cross.

www.avemariapress.com

Paperback: ISBN-13 978-1-59471-634-8

E-book: ISBN-13 978-1-59471-635-5

Cover image © Stocksy.com.

Cover and text design by Katherine Robinson.

Printed and bound in the United States of America.

Library of Congress Cataloging-in-Publication Data
Names: Wagner, Elizabeth (Sister)
Title: Seasons in my garden : meditations from a hermitage / Elizabeth Wagner.
Description: Notre Dame : Ave Maria Press, 2016.
Identifiers: LCCN 2015039222 | ISBN 9781594716348 (pbk.) | ISBN 9781594716355 (e-book)
Subjects: LCSH: Wagner, Elizabeth (Sister) | Women hermits--Maine--Windsor--Biography. | Gardeners--Religious life. | Gardens--Religious aspects--Christianity.
Classification: LCC BX4705.W223 A3 2016 | DDC 242--dc23
LC record available at http://lccn.loc.gov/2015039222

Contents

prologue: my call to the garden

Seasons of My Life

When I was a child I loved to play under the wild hemlock tree at the edge of our yard, beyond the careful symmetry of the blue spruces planted all in a row at the edge of the lawn. I spent endless hours playing there under its sweeping, graceful green branches. Sometimes my little brother joined me, but mostly I played alone. I loved its carpet of tiny, soft, brown fallen hemlock needles. The roots were mountain ridges when I dreamed of being an Aztec princess; the clefts between them were the deep valleys. It was an enchanted place.

When I was a little older, perhaps about eight or ten, the hemlock came down one night in a huge storm of rain and wind.

My safe refuge, my giant friend, my playfellow, was suddenly gone. It lay outstretched in death, its roots all torn up in a huge, flat, shallow crust of root and earth and bits of rock.

Still my dreams continued, but now they came from books. *To Kill a Mockingbird* was all the rage, and I dreamed of becoming a lawyer, working hard for the poor, the unjustly accused, the innocent.

And then I went to high school, where I felt awkward and alone, a farm girl who loved books, long solitary walks, and conversations about politics with a few friends. Maybe others beyond my circle liked these things, too, but if so, they didn't talk about them. Nor did I. I knew I was supposed to like boys (well, that was okay!) and loud music and parties and sports, and surreptitious smoking in the girls' room. I tried hard to fit into all this, and sometimes I even almost convinced myself I did fit in; but in truth, it was deadly. All that peer pressure that kids exert on one another can be fatal if you don't fit.

This alone wouldn't have been so bad if I had another mold to fit into. But what mold? What shape? I wasn't raised Catholic, or even religious, though I was sporadically sent to Sunday school. I'd never heard of monastics or monasteries. I'm not sure I even realized there was such a thing as the Catholic Church, at least not until one was built in our town when I was in junior high. Even then, all I knew were old bits of foolishness, and nothing of the reality.

So my dreams continued, safely locked in my head, far away from the scornful gaze of peers and family. Then in my senior year I stumbled into a course on the intellectual history of Europe. There were only eleven students, and I wasn't bored. Even better, I was challenged. It was an intellectual awakening for me, and something more.

The teacher was Catholic, an adult convert who taught as if ideas were important, as if they counted for something. He was a teacher whose faith influenced him, and while he never proselytized, it was clear that he had a sympathy for matters of faith and spirit. While speaking with me one day, he offered me a book about a saint, a great contemplative saint, Teresa of Avila. I was captivated, entranced, overwhelmed! My heart opened, my dreams expanded, and I knew my calling.

Unfortunately, there was more to it than that. I'd fallen in love with a dream of contemplative life, but there were some major hurdles—such as not being Catholic, not thinking I actually believed in God, not having any idea of how to find a monastery or how to enter. Not to mention that I was signed up to go off to college.

One BA later, I was still struggling, still on a roller coaster riding up the hill of faith and plummeting down the valley into no faith. I signed up for a Protestant seminary, foolishly thinking these issues could be decided by reason alone. Blessedly, the seminary taught me how to read the scriptures, and while there, the silent times I spent in the little Catholic church at the foot of the hill opened my heart to God. I was finally caught, and God reeled me in.

Convinced of my vocation, I soon entered a Carmelite monastery. Although my years in Carmel were a time of great difficulty, I loved contemplative life wholeheartedly. It was my dream, and I seemed to be living it. But the difficulties became too great, and shortly before it was time to profess solemn vows, I came to realize that God was calling me to leave. It felt incomprehensible yet clearly true.

I left, but I was bereft. Like that great hemlock, I felt cut off at my roots, upended. At first I thought I would return. But as the months turned into a year, and then two, a new awareness dawned. I realized that I wouldn't return to that particular monastery. Then, I came to see that I wouldn't return to Carmel at all. I still believed in my dream of contemplative life, but I also knew I needed an older, broader, and richer tradition than that of Carmel. Benedictine life, which had attracted me even before I entered Carmel, gradually reasserted its appeal. But where could I go to live it?

I looked at various communities over the course of several years, but in truth, I felt called to none of them. Desperate to breathe the deeper air of contemplative life, I decided to live in solitude as a hermit.

And so I came to be a hermit—by default. I was suddenly transplanted into solitude and into Maine. Though I sought the life of solitude, I didn't come to Maine gladly. In fact, I came kicking and screaming: "This is Siberia, Lord!" I came to Maine because it was a place where I could earn a living in solitude. It also had a loose network of other solitaries, so there was a certain amount of companionship and support. There was a congenial place to live in the former chaplain's apartment on the property of a tiny monastery. And yet, for me, it felt as if I'd been exiled to Siberia.

Siberia? I felt as if I'd fallen off the edge of the world.

It was unmapped terrain spiritually, too. Suddenly I was no longer a member—not even a member-in-formation—of an extremely prestigious international contemplative order. Suddenly, I was a hermit. A nobody. Living on my own, in what felt to me, at the time, like a nowhere state. While I'd never been rich, suddenly I was living hand to mouth, and just barely surviving. I was living my dream, but at the time it felt like a nightmare.

At the same time, I seemed to have nothing to hang on to, and no roots deep enough to provide nourishment and stability. My contemplative horizons and all means of "measuring" my life with God were gone. The other solitaries were helpful, but I instinctively knew I was seeking religious life in a way they were not. I floundered desperately, hoping beyond hope in my calling, my dream, and clinging to God's promises of steadfast love and presence. It always seemed to be a journey into the dark and unknown future, a pioneer journey, in which I often felt overwhelmed by the enormity of the world, and how different it is to have a calling to solitude and prayer.

Hardest of all for me was the very uniqueness of it. It was my calling, my vision, and nobody else's. I felt as though I was taking baby steps into black nothingness. I longed to blend into the crowd, but there was no crowd to blend into. But I could only keep pursuing this dream, this journey of constantly following God into the unknown. And God kept leading.

In truth, each of us has a dream. Like Abraham, we all journey in faith without a road map. Each of us is called in a unique way, and each of us must respond. But we also need to be sure it's the right dream for us. How do we do this? We ask God's help, turning to God and entreating God to show us the path that is right for us and to keep us from the wrong path. We share our dream with the appropriate people. We learn from others who have followed their own unique callings.

And so it was with me. I had a dream of solitude and prayer. It was the right dream, but not completely right, for I also loved and sought community. For a long time I thought it was not to be found, not for me. But today I am once more a member of a community, a tiny, semieremitical one. Few in numbers, we struggle with many things: limited resources, the challenges of living together in authentic prayer and relationships, and the reality that we are still nobodies in the world and generally forgotten by the Church at large. But we are living our dream, and so we are blessed.

I hope these reflections will inspire you to follow your own dream. Many threads weave in and out of them, not least of which is my own experience of following my call. It is in many ways unique to me. Yet, I hope and trust that I have scraped away enough inessentials to get down to bedrock —that is, the universal experiences common to us all: hope, trust, sadness, awareness, love.

While my life's journey has taken a road unfamiliar to many—at least in its externals—in the land of emotions, needs, and desires, I trust you will find it home turf. Each reflection, in some form, deals with human desire and human struggle, with human weakness and vulnerability. Each, I believe, speaks in some form of hope. Perhaps they are mere slivers of hope, but at times slivers are all we have.

There is another experience as well, which may not be common to all, at least not in the form expressed here. These reflections speak of the experience of God's presence, abiding with us, and woven into the texture of our days, often in unexpected and inexplicable ways. I believe this is a universal experience. But we may not all name it as God's presence. We may call it peace, or harmony, or paradise, or nirvana, or flow, or solitude. Or even darkness, or illusion. Or something else. What we call it depends on each person's own background and life story. But it is there, a hidden, elusive presence, open to those who choose to attend to it. If we do attend to it, it will lead us into our dream.

Perhaps you are hoping that this introduction will give you some background in monastic life, or in contemplation, or in prayer, or even in Catholicism. But I think it best for you to sink or swim for yourself. What you need to know will be given you. What you don't know will, I hope, provoke some tantalizing questions—questions that will lead you on and on to, as St. John of the Cross said, "I don't know what." To mystery, perhaps. To your dream. To the "more" that is greater than any words can express.

I have a word for you as you begin this book: read at your own pace. Skip around if you choose. Slow down. Speed up. Most of all, ask questions. Ask them of yourself, of your life, of God.

I have a prayer for you also, and it is this: may you always have questions, more questions than answers. May you always have a dream. And may you always find Presence weedily growing through the sunshine and the hurricanes of your days.

winter

gifts of christmas

On December 21, in the early afternoon, it began to snow. It snowed ferociously for about twelve hours, and the next morning we woke up to cold, howling winds and about a foot and a half of new snow. When I ventured out to the post office with a few late fruitcake orders, the outer field was a whiteout of blowing snow; the roads were slick and icy.

By Christmas Eve day, we were heading into another storm, though only a small one. The air was milder but still below freezing. In the late afternoon, it began to sleet and rain lightly. A walk out through the woods and field to the mailbox was an adventure of ice and sleet. As I reached my goal, a neighbor slowly drove up and braked to turn into his driveway, skidding and sliding as he did so.

No Midnight Mass for us this year, I thought, the roads are just too treacherous.

Still, the late afternoon dusk was seductive, even with sleet. Mild enough so that the cold didn't bite, sleeting only very lightly, the growing dusk was more a gradual deepening of the gray and foggy day. This late afternoon there was no one around, no one on the roads; everyone was safe at home preparing for Christmas. The outer garden was lovely: peach and cherry trees stark against the winter white, dried stalks of perennials stiff and brown. Solitary, enclosed in the fog, the trees and shrubs—even creation itself—seemed as it were to be still and hushed, hardly breathing, awaiting the birth of the Lord.

Back inside, Christmas Eve was upon us. Cleaning was finished, and the tree was up in the gathering room with lights on, though not yet decorated. Sr. Bernadette had worked her magic in the chapel: white lights, red poinsettias, the violet candles of Advent banished for another year, replaced with the clear white of Christmas. Beneath the tabernacle was the crèche, garnished with woven strands of fluffy white *miscanthus*, red winterberry, and tiny white lights. Evergreens—fir, pine, and spruce—all made an inviting backdrop, a green sanctuary for the Holy Family. On the windowsills perched the shepherds and kings, awaiting their time to approach the manger. Dusk had deepened into the early night of one of the shortest days of the year; it was time for the first Vespers of Christmas.

We don't have great or even good voices, so our singing isn't very spectacular. "Lo, How a Rose" is a challenge, but somehow we do it. The antiphons and psalms of Christmas are so familiar, so deeply loved, yet still so new and fresh each year. Perhaps that is already one of the great gifts of Christmas: the newness of it all, when it is always the same. "The King of Peace has shown himself in glory," proclaims the first antiphon. "All the peoples desire to see him."

Do I desire to see him? Yes, I do. Though at this moment of Vespers, perhaps *see* is not the operative word. This holy, simple, beautiful, loving space, so warm and enfolding, proclaims his presence. Word and song proclaim his presence. This hermitage, this community gathered here in prayer, proclaims and resonates with his life-giving breath. The gathering dusk, the stillness, all proclaim— indeed shout aloud—that he is here with us. Seeing is for the next life; here and now, at least for this moment, is already permeated with his reality.

"Behold," proclaims St. Bernard in the Office of Readings for Christmas, "peace no longer promised, but conferred; no longer delayed, but given; no longer predicted, but bestowed. Behold, God the Father has sent down to earth as it were a bag filled with his mercy; a bag to be rent open in the passion so that our ransom which it concealed might be poured out; a small bag indeed, but full. It is indeed a small child who is given to us, but in whom dwells all the fullness of the Godhead."

"The word of God, born of the Father before time began, humbled himself today for us and became human." Vespers continues as the joy of the Magnificat echoes in our tiny chapel; and then we begin the intercessions. We linger here, offering prayers for so many gifts, so many graces: prayers for friends; benefactors who have been so abundantly gracious to us; for our poor, bleeding, torn, wounded world; for our families; our local church; our community. Prayers for all traveling on slick roads, all who work on downed power lines. We pray for the hungry, lost, and homeless, and for all the gifts of the year past, even all its struggles and difficulties. There are so many prayers, so much praise, such depth of peace and gratitude.

We linger, not restless for once. It is so good to be here, to remain in this little chapel that tonight opens wide into the stable of Bethlehem and into the stable that is the world.

And then we go back to various quiet tasks as the night falls—I continue to decorate the tree while listening to carols. We wrap gifts, the simplest of gifts for one another, and for the animals. A can of dog food for Daisy Mae, a bag of kitty treats for Sophronius. I amuse myself with making rhyming enclosures for the gifts, playfully hoping to tease: "If what's inside does not gratify; Gloria Jean's will satisfy" written on a container of coffee.

Because of the slick roads, tonight we will pray Vigils in place of Midnight Mass. Daisy Mae is the first one into the chapel. She clearly wonders why we are up way past her bedtime, and stretches out on the carpet, ready to enjoy a nap. Prayer and praise continue, as we celebrate the birth of Emmanuel, God's presence here among us. God is indeed here among us this night, and our hearts are filled with gratitude and wonder and peace.

The next morning is bright, clear, and extremely windy; the storm has blown out into the Maritimes. Setting out for Mass, we are relaxed, quiet, still filled with Christmas peace. About three miles from church, as we drive through an undeveloped patch of woods, we are stunned as a huge, old white pine, Maine's signature tree, snaps off and crashes across the road, not fifty feet from where we come to a quick stop. Electric wires bounce and crash also, but fortunately not on the car. We are stunned; my mouth drops open, and I feel temporarily paralyzed from shock. Then I back up, pull off, find the cell phone, and dial 911. The woman first wants to be sure we are okay, asks what road we are on, then asks where the tree is, precisely. Are there any landmarks? I look around, "Well, there are lot of trees," I offer weakly.

"How will they know where it is?" she asks.

"They'll know because they can't drive any farther," I reply.

We take deep breaths, turn around, and find another way to St. Denis, arriving just in time for Mass. We are past the homily and into the creed before the adrenalin in my system finally starts slowing down, and I can pay attention. Even then, the giant tree majestically crashes down over and over in my head. After Mass, we greet friends, share the story, exclaim over our close call, and wish one another a merry Christmas.

And then at home, and finally peeling vegetables and preparing dinner, I reconnect with the peace and joy of the day. It is a homegrown dinner, using nearly the last of our garden's produce. With these lovely fruits of the garden, and so much quiet time for prayer, it is an opportunity to pause with all the creatures gathered at the crib, and just quietly give thanks.

Yet, how strange a contrast it is that in the midst of this ocean of prayer and praise and deep peace there was this terrifying and intrusive exclamation point, the crashing of a massive tree. Another second or two and we would have been crushed under its weight. What is this about, I wonder; what meaning could it possibly have? How to reconcile it with the peaceful serenity of the day?

Reflecting on it, I ponder the meaning of Christmas itself. A child is born for us. A child who brings "good news," news of "peace on earth, goodwill to all." This a child who brings peace, who brings praise, who brings wonder and joy and gratitude. So, in limited measure, does every child. And like every child, this child is vulnerable. In the midst of this seemingly peaceful birth, there are disquieting signs, indications of trauma. His parents are poor, and the only place for his birth is with the animals, in a stable. Immediately after his birth his parents are forced to flee to protect this child from being killed. A refugee from his own country, this child, like every child, is at risk.

Maybe this is the connection between the two extremes, for at all times, whether in peace or in terror, we are vulnerable. How much easier to forget our vulnerability when we're at peace! Things don't seem to affect us as much, or perhaps our feet are on firmer psychic ground. Yet, the truth is that every human being, every creature on earth, even the earth itself, is vulnerable. A great tree, growing into maturity over long decades, is suddenly brought low by a huge wind. Human creatures, peacefully cocooned in a good, safe car, are suddenly brought to a screeching halt, and made vividly aware of how very fragile they are. A tiny newborn, the most vulnerable of all creatures, is taken by its parents as they flee to save his life.

Our faith reminds us that *this* newborn is God; omnipotent God, the "wonder-counselor, mighty God, Prince of Peace." Yet, he was still a vulnerable, helpless newborn. The One who grants us whatever peace we might enjoy in this life is also the One who allows himself to be so terribly, completely helpless. When grown to adulthood he was still vulnerable, even entering into the ultimate helplessness of death.

Vulnerability might well be the hallmark of all creation. Huge trees are vulnerable to sudden gusts of wind; gardens are vulnerable to too much water, to a lack of water, to all sorts of pests and diseases. Our beautiful, fragile earth is so very vulnerable: to climate change, to global warming, to environmental degradation. Tiny infants and children are at risk from abuse, neglect, famine, poverty, war. And so are adults.

And in spite of all the vulnerability, all the terror, all the horror, there is still peace, at least at times. Could it be that peace is what makes it possible for us to allow ourselves to be vulnerable, and still carry on? Christmas is pure gift: the gift of Emmanuel, God become incarnate, the God who brings us such depth of peace. Perhaps it is only in

God, the ever peaceful One, that we are empowered to embrace our helplessness, our poverty, our
finite createdness. In peace, we can allow ourselves
to be, and allow others to be. In peace, we can allow
huge trees to come crashing down, and know that
God is still with us, because God has entered our
world: Jesus has been born for us. Jesus has peacefully embraced vulnerability and is with us in it.
The fall of the tree was only a small, brief incident
in our unfolding day—though it took on a much
greater magnitude through the depth and urgency
of our shock and fear. Yet, it was bracketed, so to
speak, enclosed and enfolded in the parentheses of
peacefulness.

"Hungry is he who nourished unnumbered
thousands, toiling is he who refreshes the toilers; he
has nowhere to lay his head but controls all things
by his hand; he suffers and yet heals all sufferings;
he is buffeted by blows and presents the world with
freedom; he is pierced in his side and restores the
side of Adam." So we read in the breviary for January 8.

Jesus entered into hunger and thirst, sickness
and suffering, limitation, poverty, and even death.
In his peace, we, too, can enter into our own limitations, vulnerability, and sufferings—even our
own death. We are empowered to embrace the little, everyday deaths, as well as the big one when
we are called to let go of this life and enter into a
greater life with God.

Writing this now, after Christmas, here in Maine we are in the depth of winter. The bitter cold of January is upon us. Several snowstorms have dropped their white burden. The cloister garden is gradually losing its shape under smooth white billows. In the outer garden, the peach trees and cherry trees still stand stark, but the perennials are now covered over with snow. I try to remember that all this snow is good for the garden, a blanket of white insulation that keeps the plants firmly rooted in the frozen earth.

Winds blow, trees fall, winter's harshness is long and wearying. Yet, peacefulness is a gift that may spring up anytime, anywhere. Peacefulness was given to us through the Incarnation. Peaceful gifts of Christmas remind us of the One who is with us, even when large trees—or our entire world— come crashing down around us.

bare bones

The trunks and branches of the bare trees shimmer in the winter sun. It is a glorious winter day, sunny, bright, and cold, with a blue, cloudless sky—the best of winter.

The roads are clear, so it's a day for getting out to do errands. I'm returning from Winslow, alone in the car, on an empty road. The sun on the bare bones of the trees is magnificent: austere poetry in tan, brown, gray, and black trunks, with white snow and blue shadow, and everywhere, sunlight.

Old apple trees are gnarled and twisted, with dark gray bark and a few old barn-red apples, shriveled and shrunken, still hanging from the boughs. A magnificent elm, one of the few healthy specimens I've seen, its vase shape unmistakable, its gray, furrowed trunk tall and straight. Huge

maples grace the front of a classic old Maine farm-
house. They are so old that their lower branches are
as big around as many other trees. Some of these
great trees are dying. Parts of them are rotted away,
just mighty ancient trunks, with one or two enormous branches still remaining.

Occasionally there are entrancing clusters of
white birch, though the true white birch is rare
here. Like other birches, they are bare, but showing
hints of next year's seeds at each delicate fingertip.

There are fir and spruce and hemlock, too.
Conifers don't bare their bones but remain dis-
creetly clad in green throughout the year. I sur-
mise it's because their structure isn't so lovely:
just straight up for the central trunk, and straight
out for the branches. Eastern white pines are the
exception to this rule. Once full-grown and mature,
they are magnificent, rugged specimens, each with
its own personality and character. Still clothed in
green, they nonetheless have lots of bone showing:
massive trunks and lower branches, huge knots
and twists and divisions. Each one is unique, yet
each is so obviously white pine.

The real dazzlers, to my mind, are the mature
oaks. With rugged brown trunks, huge spreading
branches growing out fairly low from the trunk,
other branches of all sizes and shapes burgeon-
ing out in every direction, each one is completely
unique, its personality distinctive. Forged into
character by their site, their soil, and the weather,
they are mute witnesses to the power of life and
endurance. The paradox of massive trunks and
branches with the sensitive tracery of thousands

of individual twigs stops my breath with wonder. Highlighted by sunlight, outlined against blue sky and shadow and brilliant white snow, they are heartbreakingly beautiful.

The next morning, the delicate filigree of black branches, backlit by the rose and pink of the pre-dawn sunrise, fills my eyes and heart as I sit in my cell for morning *lectio divina* (sacred reading). The bare bones of winter trees surround me with spaciousness, much as the horarium of our monastic day provides the bare bones of structure that opens out into the spaciousness of God.

Our horarium gives us time, and our building the space, for solitude. Our chapel is a simple, spare room that holds two plain benches where we sit for community prayer four times each day. A tiny Shaker-style table serves as both lectern and altar. The focus of the room is the tabernacle, centered on the east wall. Here are a few icons, a central rug. Four large windows overlooking the view fill this empty space with sunlight, the pale reflection of the Presence that abides here among us.

The structure of our day gives us Vigils, Lauds, Vespers, and Compline together in the chapel daily. These four offices with their recurring rhythms of psalms, readings, and prayer form the structure that leads to and supports our solitary prayer: those quiet hours, each morning and evening, during which we can be alone with the Lord.

My cell is where I sit in solitude, morning after morning, evening after evening, for prayer, meditation, and lectio. Here I sit, here where I can just be, and be still, in the presence of the One who loves me beyond all others. Here is the space of encounter with this presence, this gracious empty space whose structure is four walls, a floor, a ceiling, a few simple pieces of furniture—but whose horizon is infinity. This space encompasses eternity in the here and now of daily life.

Infinite horizons, however, are not always spacious, however paradoxical that might seem, and the cell can seem to press down on me and hem me in. The cell is so very often the place of struggle and combat. "The spiritual combat of the desert" it is called, and some days it feels as though all the combat of the entire world has taken up residence in my cell—even worse, in my own heart and mind. "Every day I am waging warfare," a monastic friend once said.

Daily life at its most basic, stripped to its bare bones, consists of two movements. One is combative, polarizing, stretching us in seemingly opposite directions at the same moment. The other is peace-filled, integrating, grounding. I never know which way any particular day will go.

The challenge in solitude, as in every life, is to retain that horizon of infinite spaciousness, when mind and heart, and even the events of daily life, conspire to convince me that my only horizon is the confines of myself. This is the battle that all of us wage. In the cloister, however, we are rarely distracted from it, and so it looms enormously large. Slowly learning our own weaknesses and disabilities, our own particular proneness to negativity of whatever sort, we spend a lifetime learning how to counteract ourselves.

The last two days have been chock-full of struggle. Anger and irritation are rampant. I cannot chase them away, no matter how I try. Finally I remember that I'm very tired and pressured. There is too much to do, and not quite enough time. I finally remember that fatigue and pressure always have this effect. The tiniest difficulties loom as major life-threatening obstacles. The mere recollection that I'm tired and stressed is the beginning of a graced movement away from focusing on myself and into the gracious expansiveness of God's presence.

Monastic life does not have many distractions, and this is not by chance. But it can surely make for struggle. Distractions can help us move beyond our immediate need or difficulty: we become aware that others have even greater difficulties, or we get absorbed in something and forget ourselves, or we get busy and forget ourselves. Distractions can give us enough inner space to gain perspective.

But often distractions lead not to a proper forgetfulness of self but to the kind of forgetfulness that is oblivion. Distractions can be the kiss of death. We can distract ourselves with so many things: food, sleep, TV and movies, shopping, the latest gadgets, the Internet, and on and on and on—not to mention the really destructive distractions: cigarettes, alcohol, drugs.

Like the stripped-down trees, monastic life has few distractions so that we can attend to the one thing necessary: the all-important and ever-present relationship with God. Many never consciously advert to this relationship. Yet, some do, and especially at more profound moments of their lives. Recently a friend described to me the last few weeks and days of her husband's struggle with a brain tumor. "At the end," she said, "all he had left was breathing and love."

Breathing and love: that could be a description of what our life is meant to be about. After all, what is the point of this life? Why would anyone willingly subject herself to such a stripped-down life, such an existence of struggle? For each of us, the answer is unique; yet, for all of us, there are two common elements, two dimensions, each of them a slow centrifugal dance around this reality we call love.

Sometime in her life, each person called to this monastic life has fallen head over heels in love. Fallen so deeply in love that she wants to live with the loved one every day of her life. So much in love that she can only listen to the words of one person: the One she loves. "Lord, you have the words of eternal life" (Jn 6:68).

"You have seduced me, Lord, and I let myself be seduced," says Jeremiah (Jer 20:7). *Seduction* is not too strong a word. We are seduced by desire for God, and set in motion by this attraction. Desire for God is the foundation of monastic life, the foundation of solitude. "Late have I loved you, O beauty so ancient and so new," lamented St. Augustine, "late have I loved you." Each of us can witness to this. No matter how young we were when we were attracted to God, it was never young enough. Monastic life is the search for God, says Benedict.

We listen, we seek, we follow, we struggle, perpetually attracted by desire for God.

"On my bed at night I sought him whom my soul loves—I sought him but found him not. I called him, but he gave no answer. I will rise now and go about the city; in the streets and in the squares; I will seek him whom my soul loves" (Sg 3:1–2). This is the first reading for the feast of St. Mary Magdalene, the one who sat at the Lord's feet, seduced by the attraction of his words. She is the icon and archetype of all those whose calling is contemplative life. "You shall love the Lord your God with all your heart, and with all your soul, and with all your strength, and with all your mind" (Lk 10:27). Such a love implies struggle, and surrender, and simplicity: the movement away from self-love.

And the other face of love wells up from the first: the outward movement, counterpoise of the love of the infinitely attractive One: "And your neighbor as yourself" (Lk 10:27b). Love is the motive force that drives this second principle of contemplative life. Love for neighbor, love for all God's world. Our neighbor is always held close in our hearts and in our prayer. Intercessory prayer has sometimes been scoffed at. How impossible to prove that it gets results! After all, our society is all about proof and materially verifiable facts. How difficult a question it is theologically! After all, if God already knows what we need, why do we bother to ask? Yet, how impossible it is to *disprove* it to someone who has felt the efficacy of another's intercession to God! Love for neighbor includes: those we know and those we don't know: the sisters

with whom we live, the unknown neighbors who
suffer and struggle and die on the other side of the
world. Love for neighbor, prayer for neighbor—this
is the other face of contemplative life.

And yet, it is all hidden; the life remains
stripped to bare bones, visible to those whose eyes
can see, yet it is a life so simple and ordinary that
most eyes see through it and do not see. The Lord
whose love and whose face we seek "was sent not
only to be recognized but to remain hidden."[1] Such,
too, is contemplative life in its simplicity: recognized, and yet equally hidden.

"The house was filled with the fragrance of
the perfume" (Jn 12:3). This is John's comment on
Mary's action in breaking her jar of perfume and
anointing Jesus' feet. Here again, Mary is the icon
of contemplative love. This life so hidden and yet
so unobtrusively open: how like a fragrance it is!
Invisible, nearly imperceptible, yet a very real and
delicious something. And it fills the house with its
fragrance: the house that is our body, the house
that is the Church, the house that is the world at
large, and only perceptible to those who can deeply
breathe and take it in.

"Breathing and love," I recall. Breathing and
love—what a wonderful description of our life!
"God has given to the earth the breath which feeds
it. It is his breath that gives life to all things. And
if he were to hold his breath, everything would be
annihilated. His breath vibrates in yours, in your
voice. It is the breath of God that you breathe—
and you are unaware of it."[2] A stripped-down, bare
bones life hasn't got much left: just breathing and

love. In struggle and in peace, in darkness and in light, there are the two movements of love: breathing in, breathing out.

In winter, trees are stripped to bare bones. In contemplative life, it sometimes can seem as though it is always winter, always struggle, perpetual warfare with our very selves. Why would anyone ever want to live perpetually stripped down to basics? The only answer can be breathing and love. Bare bones, stripped-down trees, the harsh struggle of winter—these trees, beautiful in their simplicity, are stripped to receive the gift of springtime love.

blessed boredom

"Sit in your cell, and your cell will teach you everything."[1] This famous aphorism of Abba Moses, the
fourth-century Egyptian hermit, could well have
been written for January in Maine, where sitting
in one's cell is often the only option. A week ago
another major snowstorm dumped over a foot of
snow. Since then, we've had bitter cold. Except for
excursions to the chapel, community room, and
refectory, all I can do is sit in my cell. Even worse,
I've aggravated an old knee injury, so I don't dare
put on snowshoes and take a walk down the prayer
trail.

And so I sit today and gaze outdoors: a beautiful day, bright and sunny, but bitter cold. I see
the beech boughs waving in the brisk northwest
wind; I see the buds for next year's growth at their

tips. A long time before those buds will unfurl! Occasional snow devils, kicked up by the wind, whirl around the old blueberry field. The snow is blindingly white. The pines look cold in the wind; their needles are pinched and shriveled. The juniper looks unfazed, much of it snow covered. The white trunks of the birch soak up the white of the snow and give it off with dazzling clarity. Behind the building to the west, chickadees and finches perch precariously on the larch cones, digging out the seeds. Unbelievably, a small flock of robins has wintered over; I see them occasionally flying between beech and apple.

In the cloister garden, the snow is piled high. A friend raked the snow off the cloister roof, and the only place for it to go was right onto the garden. Even the statues at the four corners of the garden are mostly covered. A few of the roses still poke through the snow mounds, along with some of the tallest perennials. The faded brown stalks are a focal point, a contrast to the endless billows of white.

The gathering room, our all-purpose area that holds refectory, library, and community room, is sheer joy. Here the windows face south and west and flood the room with light and sun all winter long. Our little monastery was only recently built, so we were able to use many recent construction advantages: super insulation, passive solar orientation, and radiant heat in the floor. Though today is bitter outdoors, the brilliant sun keeps the room snug and warm.

This is a gracious space, with a cathedral ceiling, massive beams, clerestory windows, and book-lined walls. My most precious herbs perch on black benches in front of the large south windows, soaking up the sunshine. A huge rosemary, a bay, a lavender, lemon grass, and myrtle all love this space. Two over-wintering parsleys, country cousins of the other elegant herbs, sit dowdily nearby. The sun turns the sword leaves of the lemon grass into translucent, living green. No geraniums got potted up last fall, so there are no flowers. But even without bright color, the green reality of the plants reminds me that winter will pass, and beneath the snow, the earth awaits.

"The changing seasons form the crucible in which we experience time on earth."[2] So says Baron Wormser, a former Maine poet laureate.

Winter in Maine is truly a crucible: a slow chalice of transformation. One is pushed deep down into oneself by the weight of winter; long, snowy days; long snow-covered months. Bitter, icy cold, with winds whipping right down off the Arctic Circle, or so it feels. In the bitterest of the cold there is usually sunshine—delusional sunshine, bright and splendid, but without the merest whiff of warmth. The cold yields to clouds and milder temperatures, but with the clouds comes snow—often, lots of snow, as in the last storm. Last winter we had interminable snow; it seemed eternal, and the continual gray overcast grew more and more depressing as the winter progressed.

And so I sit in my cell, and gaze out. "Boredom," I think, "this is boredom." Yet, I have more than enough to keep me busy. Some task or other

always needs to be done. There's lots of computer
and office work. There's cleaning and shoveling
and sometimes cooking, and making sure the house
runs well. There is the usual routine of prayer, both
in community and in solitude. There are the twice-
weekly Communion services for the parish. There
is fundraising for our longed-for retreat house,
and planning for it. There are people to see, and
seemingly unending correspondence. There is at
the moment a deluge of potential vocation appli-
cants. Most, perhaps all, will never pan out. But
all must be attended to, listened to, corresponded
with. Some will even visit. One or more, God willing, might even enter.

Seed catalogs have arrived, with their tempting listings and flashy colors. Even flashier e-mail
advertisements from two of my favorite suppliers
show up. One, from a famous East Coast nursery,
sends regular tantalizing ads every Sunday. Today's
installment features colorful and tasteful combina-
tions of annuals for summer planters, an inviting
show of color in a black and white month. Another,
from a much-loved homegrown Maine company,
brings a monthly calendar filled with useful and
user-friendly garden information.

Normally by late January I have already pondered over what new plants to try, planned the garden, and ordered the seeds. All the usual ones, plus
a couple of new ones that intrigue, or that might
look good in the garden. Or a new variety of vegetable. Or something extra, "just for fun."

So far I've ordered a few trees and shrubs, set
for pickup in late April. But otherwise, nothing. I

look at the seed catalogs, and yawn. Boredom has set in.

Winter is a crucible indeed: a great white bowl holding all the elements for transformation. It is a large kettle, whose sides are the walls of the hermitage and the cold harsh winter that surrounds it. The fire is the pressure of being disconnected from the face of the earth—no brown soil, no green grass, no rich smell of earth. And the lid? Boredom, and the long months of waiting for new life. My only lullaby of spring is a few green herbs on a black bench in the sun.

One of the things I have learned over the years is that the feelings I am experiencing are a good indication of how to find God's voice in my life. They are the living evidence of the word God is speaking to me right here and now. In order to hear God speaking in this way, I need to "listen with the ear of my heart," as the *Rule* tells me. I must be still, pay attention, and ask questions. "Go deeper," I hear. "Go deeper." Go deep, with the earth, with the plants, with the living things. Go deep, be still, and in the stillness, listen. Boredom would have me move away and distract myself. Instead I am called to sit in my cell, be still, and listen.

I read the daily scriptures, praying with them. Today I read the call of Peter and Andrew, James and John. Speaking loud and clear to me is a seemingly peripheral line, "believe in the gospel" (Mk 1:15 NAB). "Believe in the gospel," I repeat, over and over, breathing in and out, "believe in the gospel." Slowly, heart and mind quiet. I remember that *gospel* means "good news." Unutterably good news, so very good that we find it nearly impossible to even take it in, much less believe it. Believe in the good news.

Amazingly, we have lots of ordinary, everyday good news right now. We are having extra time for prayer and solitude, and we live in a wonderful new hermitage, with minimal maintenance and minimal need for heat and power. This is a stunningly beautiful place, with views to the south and east, protected from the north and west and from the bitter winds of winter. We have solitude and spaciousness, a wonderful group of friends and supporters, and even a candidate who is planning to enter in a few months, and other potential candidates who will soon be visiting. Sure, there are daily difficulties, frustrations, troubles. But there is so much good news right now; why should I be bored?

But in fact, I am, and so God is trying to get my attention with it. Perhaps the boredom is masking something deeper? Perhaps it is the lid I've put on deeper emotions. Perhaps . . . I think back, and remember that a while ago, our new candidate indicated that she would like to enter in late April. Suddenly, after having just two members for a long time, we were faced with a possible third. Suddenly we were faced with the reality of change. Anxiety flared up, real and strong. I pondered it, wondering if it was indicating that she should not enter. No, I finally decided, it wasn't that sort of anxiety. It's the anxiety that comes with the reality of change, commitment, and new life. And then, after I decided that, it seemed to go away.

Today I realize that it hasn't gone away, I've just covered it up. God is reminding me: this anxiety is real. It's not bad and it's not overwhelming, but it is real. "Anxiety is my voice, speaking within you," God is saying. "It's telling you your life will change a bit. But remember, 'believe in the gospel,' and know that I am with you in it." It's a good change, we believe, but any change leads to the unknown. God is leading us to deeper faith, deeper trust. God leads me on my own journey in faith, and leads us together in this little house of God deeper into its God-given mission of faith and prayer. Each time we step out in faith and trust, we have the joy and hope of new life, but we also feel the cool breath of anxiety. If we didn't, we wouldn't be human. Anxiety right now is God's gift, urging caution, yet also proclaiming the imminence of new life.

January is a good time to sit in the cell and learn from it. Boredom would have us move away, into the world of distraction. Boredom would have us dissipate our energies, and turn away from attentiveness to the "one thing necessary." Yet, boredom, like any emotion, need not be acted upon. We can sit with it, pay attention to it, talk to it. Respect boredom, and it will yield to our desire to learn from it.

January is a crucible, and crucibles are all about transformation. That's a big word, yet a hopeful word. Sometimes it can seem an impossible word. The message of the seasons is that change and transformation happens. The message of the Gospel? "Believe in the good news . . . for nothing is impossible to God."

standing far off

The shortest month of the year lasts forever. In February, in the depth of winter, time stands still. The days are slowly lengthening and the dark receding, but winter persists unabated. Time hangs heavy as we wait for the spring that seems so immensely far off.

This winter is harsh, with unrelenting cold and buffeting storms. True, we have days and even a week or more at a time without a storm. But then we're hit with another nor'easter, a major storm that dumps a foot of snow or more. In between, the days are cold and gloomy. Snow piles grow ever larger. As the mounds get higher, shoveling the walkway gets harder and harder. We run out of places to put the snow and finally hire a backhoe to move the piles around and make some room in the

driveway. Worst of all, there is no bare ground anywhere, and so I feel disconnected from the earth.
My psyche craves the greenery of spring, my feet
are craving bare earth, and all I find is snow and ice.

I feel as though I am standing still. I'm
oppressed by the weather, tired from too many
projects that seem never to come to completion,
fatigued by demands on time, talents, and energy.
I can't summon any enthusiasm for prayer or lectio.
Everything is stale; nothing appeals.

Lent begins late in the month. Normally it's one
of my favorite seasons, a time of life, renewal, and
hope. Since my first year as a Catholic, Lent has
meant not a season of guilt and misery, but a wonderful time of deepening and rebirth. This winter,
life and hope seem to have migrated south, gone
with the robins and the wild geese.

Perhaps it is fatigue, perhaps it is anxiety about
change, or perhaps it is the weather. For whatever
reason, I seem to be paralyzed, unable to do more
than exist from day to day. Prayer and lectio are
boring; my relationship with God appears remote.
I can think of so many things I should be doing, so
many initiatives I should take. But can I actually get
myself going on them? No. The more I dally and
delay, the worse the paralysis feels and the more
distant God seems to be. I continue to pray, continue to practice lectio, continue my normal routine.
Yet, dejection and melancholy persist, and I teeter
at times on the verge of despair—despair of many
things but most of all myself. After all, it's not God
who is to blame for my inertia, is it?

Then one day for lectio I reread the parable of the Pharisee and the publican in Luke 18. I read aloud the familiar words and, for the first time, hear this phrase, spoken of the publican, that public disgrace: "standing far off."

Standing far off! "But the tax collector, standing far off, would not even look up to heaven, but was beating his breast and saying, 'God, be merciful to me, a sinner!'"(Lk 18:13). Always before, I had focused on the last part of that verse, but that morning three words pierced my heart: standing far off. What else had I been doing for the entire month of February but standing far off? Far off from God, far off from myself, far off from engagement with life.

God's response? "I tell you, this man went down to his home justified" (Lk 18:14). Reading this, my heart opened, and I wept. I was indeed standing far off, and yet God, who knows me well, said, "It's okay." It still doesn't feel very good, and it continues to make my life challenging, but as far as God is concerned, it's okay. Standing far off may not feel comfortable, but God understands and remains close to me in infinite compassion. Though I stand far off, God does not.

I notice that in this gospel story people are standing. At the time of Jesus and for centuries after, people would stand for prayer. Note the difference between the Pharisee and the tax collector: the Pharisee is standing *by himself* in splendid isolation. He obviously felt himself to be above and beyond the ordinary run of humanity. The Pharisee stands by himself in enormous self-righteousness. And the publican, that lowly tax collector? The publican stands *far off*, not daring to come near to God, to heaven, to the Holy One.

There are many other times when people stand in the scriptures. In Psalm 135:2 the psalmist "stand[s] in the house of the Lord, in the courts of the house of our God," an attitude of worship. There are other famous examples. Mary, the Mother of Jesus, stood near his Cross. Three days later another Mary, who came weeping to the tomb, was privileged to be the apostle to the apostles, the first great witness of the Resurrection.

All of these are concrete instances of simply *standing*. The implications of this basic posture are enormous—and enormously varied. Our stance in life says so much about who we are and how we are feeling. Mary, the Mother of Jesus, stands before her dying Son in enormous sorrow and suffering. Mary Magdalene also stands in grief and longing and sorrow, and yet her sorrow is transformed into wonder and amazement and joy.

How frequently do we all stand far off? And for so many different reasons! Like the publican, we are even unable to raise our eyes or thoughts or heart.

We stand far off in guilt over all the miserable things we have done or not done. Surely God knows our horrible sins and failings. We live in terror of condemnation. How could we dare approach the Holy One?

We stand far off in unworthiness. Perhaps we think we're too sinful. Or perhaps we know we could never live up to the standard of perfection we think God has set for us. Never mind that it is we who have set it for ourselves. Never mind that it's unattainable, too high for any human being ever to reach! Nevertheless we believe ourselves unworthy, and we stand far off, cringing in a corner, our heads bowed to earth, able only to look at our unlovely imperfection.

Perhaps we stand far off because we're afraid. After all, don't we know that God will judge us? Who can possibly stand before God's face unafraid? We read, "It is a fearful thing to fall into the hands of the living God" (Heb 10:31), and we forget the story of the good thief, forgiven on the cross. Or else we think the thief was in some way different from us, better than us, more open to God's love than we are. We stand far off, abiding in fear.

We stand far off because we feel dry, arid, and unmoved. The things of God are outside our hearts, unable to enter, and we feel we must be pushing God away. "Surely this must be my fault? Surely if I only tried harder, did something different?" So we think, and yet we are unable, and we turn away and stand far, far off.

We stand far off because we are anxious. God may not really be the loving and compassionate One of whom we have heard others speak. And there are so many other anxieties as well! "How will I pay the bills today, and will my children have the courage to turn away from peers who push them toward drugs and alcohol? Will that sick parent or spouse really get better? Will there be enough money for retirement? What will I do when I grow old? Who will take care of me? Can I really entrust God with all these worries? It seems

so unbelievable to think that God could care for me.
It really is all up to me, isn't it? How can I ever go
close to God with all this on my mind?" We stand
far off from God, but we stand very, very close to
all our worries and anxieties.

We stand far off, and sometimes we just don't
know why. Or we may not know how to move
toward God. Perhaps we feel stuck, paralyzed.

We stand far off, because we feel ashamed. Perhaps we've done something we feel is too awful to
talk about. It might not even be something all that
important—but it's horribly important to us! We
are ashamed because we eat too much, or we talk
too much. And the greatest shame of all: we don't
look good enough. Shame is so deeply connected
to our bodies and our looks, to our posture, to our
stance in the world. We are very much ashamed,
and so we hang back, hoping to be unseen, standing far off.

We hang back and stand far off when we feel
abandoned. Perhaps the deepest fear, the deepest
shame, and the deepest anxiety is about abandonment. Why would anyone ever love us or care for
us or watch over us when we're so unlovable?
Impossible! We've experienced this many times
before in our lives, haven't we? Parents and siblings let us down just when we most needed them.
Friends betrayed us; the world turned its back.
Besides, we'd rather sit in our bleak, dark isolation. We may be miserable, and we may feel dead,
as though we've turned to stone. But at least it's
familiar. It's not risky or challenging, and it doesn't

hold out any false hopes. And so we stand far, far off in our abandonment and isolation.

Abandonment! Writing this some weeks later, this word shivers through me. For so many weeks now, I have been puzzling about what this paralysis means. What is it that I am really experiencing? How it perplexes me! Today this word resonates deeply, awakening echoes that make me cringe. I've not felt disconnected, and I'm unaware of turning away from God, yet I've felt remote.

Now I begin to wonder: From whom am I standing far off? Is it from God? Or more likely, is it from myself? Could it be that I stand far off from my own deepest longings, sorrows, hopes, and fears? Surely this is the source of my paralysis! I have cut myself off from myself, taken all my energy and used it to hold myself down. I have fled from the deepest part of my own self, and now I feel disconnected.

How could this have happened without my even noticing? I wonder. I recall the weeks and even months leading up to this winter. I was busy: really, really busy. It was perhaps the busiest time in my entire life. There was little time for prayer, even less for being still. It was a time of hard work and challenges. I knew there was a fixed time limit to this busyness; I knew it wouldn't last forever. That alone made it bearable.

Then the busy time ended, and there was time to relax. But somehow, in the process, my deepest self had gone underground, as though it had died and was buried. Worst of all, it was forgotten: " I have passed out of mind like one who is dead" (Ps 31:12).

Like the dead, my inner self was so long forgotten that now my heart is numb. How can I awaken it? I take time each day for quiet; I try to pay attention to the deepest longings of my poor, dull heart. I apologize to my own deepest self for such desertion.

At times I see glimmers of hope, catch echoes of the child who still exists deep within, yet seems so withdrawn. So far these are distant murmurs only, occasional glimpses of this shy, deep self—the Deep One, I sometimes call her, for she is deep. She lives deep down within me, and she is possessed of profound insight, intuition, longings, and sorrows. Playfulness, too! She is the one abandoned by my day-to-day self, the functional, competent, organized self. The busy self. Now I try to make amends. I spend time each day just trying to be present to this deepest part of myself, this little one long forgotten, this vulnerable one who is like a thing thrown away. Occasionally she responds, and I am able to feel her presence briefly: in tears, in joy, in a sense of deep peace and connectedness. But, mostly, I seem to be sentenced to standing far off.

Alienated from myself, I am alienated from God. Close to myself—my entire self, not just the competent, functional self—I am close to the One who stands close to me.

Speaking recently with a friend, I recalled that our faith does not exempt us from suffering. Yet, this same faith reminds me that in Jesus the Christ, God has entered into our humanity. God has embraced our struggles, sufferings, and sorrows and has taken on our bodilyness, neediness, and vulnerability, even our failings. Standing with us in all things, he is even named Emmanuel, God *with* us. We may be standing far off, but Jesus stands close by.

I remember this now as I lament my inner standoff. It is clear that I need to learn how to come close to my deep and most vital self again. Perhaps this difficult time is the prelude to the dawn of a deeper intimacy with both self and God. Meanwhile I need to learn from the One who stands so completely with me. I must learn how to be close, how to comfort, how to be present, and all the while how to be respectful of this deeper self.

Perhaps we are all like this. Perhaps we are all lost, alienated, standing far off from ourselves and from God. Perhaps we all must work at coming close. Perhaps intimacy, even with ourselves, never comes easily. I call upon my faith, reminding myself of God's past actions and constant loving presence. I know God is with me, standing close by, even though I do not always feel that loving peacefulness.

Standing far off, I remain in the desert this February. I call upon the living One, and remind myself that God is always standing close at hand.

qoheleth's paradox

Like a biting March wind, the insights and wisdom of Qoheleth, that ancient wisdom writer in Israel, pierce us with their mood of negativity and weariness. Like that same March day, he also can be filled with sunshine. Even as March weather is filled with alternate turns, first toward winter, then toward spring, so Qoheleth in one line speaks of the futility of life, and in another of its pleasures and joy.

This year's March is the climax of a long, harsh, infinitely wearying winter. Maine has been pounded with storm after storm. And so we are weary this March, very weary of weather and storms. My inner world mirrors the outer, for my thoughts are diffuse, chaotic, and conflicting. Thought jostles thought in rapid succession, as storm piles pell-mell upon storm. Nowhere do I find peace or cessation from this wearying, unending parade.

Perhaps Qoheleth was weary, too. Scripture scholars tell us he lived in a difficult time, when Israel lived under foreign rulers and masters, with high taxation, with the old ties of family and tribe falling apart, and with a new class consciousness based on wealth coming into being. Maybe Qoheleth had been trying to maintain his life according to the old ways of the wisdom tradition: fear the Lord, do what is right, and you will be rewarded with a good life. Yet, he couldn't help noticing that this didn't always seem to work. "I saw under the sun that in the place of justice, wickedness was there, and in the place of righteousness, wickedness was there as well" (Eccl 3:16).

I, too, see the injustice and inequity in life, especially at times when events conspire to overthrow me. My perceptions change like the March wind, skittering around to the north, blowing cold across my mind with anger, cynicism, and doubt.

I join Qoheleth in his constant refrain about life: "Vanity of vanities, all is vanity" (Eccl 1:2; 12:8). This word "vanity" held so many shades of meanings for him. It signified a puff of air, a breath, or vapor. It meant something insubstantial, ephemeral: something vain or futile. Perhaps "ephemeral" is the critical word, for much of what Qoheleth says points out the transitory nature of life. Life is fleeting, he seems to say, and always at its end comes death. "For the fate of humans and the fate of animals is the same; as one dies, so dies the other. All go to one place, all are from the dust, and all turn to dust again" (Eccl 3:19–20). For Qoheleth death is the end. There is no afterlife, and so death is a particularly final reality. This universal presence of death recurs again and again in Qoheleth, and often in myself as well, a constant refrain highlighting the evanescence of life, and questioning its worth and value.

Paradoxically, this same presence of death highlights the joys of life and the goodness of creation, much as the difficulty and harshness of a Maine winter gives added joy and gladness to the first hints of spring. For another continual refrain is: "This is what I have seen to be good: it is fitting to eat and drink and find enjoyment in all the toil with which one toils under the sun the few days of the life God gives us; for this is our lot" (Eccl 5:18). While the constant repetition of this theme is the counterpoint to the refrain of "vanity of vanity," this counterpoint never seems quite strong enough to counterbalance the weariness of Qoheleth's skeptical mood of doubt.

Eating, drinking, working, even life itself— these are God's good gifts, and they should be enjoyed, as Qoheleth says. We cannot hold on to them forever, for death will take them from us. But while we are alive, we should rejoice in what we have. In fact, we should rejoice in each present moment, for this is all we have, and it is a gift from God. If we would only relax our mind's possessive grasp on future and past, and ease off our constant comparison with others, each present moment could blossom for us into receptivity to God's gracious gifts.

Perhaps Qoheleth was unaware of this inner attitude, for he seems preoccupied only with what happens in the world, and with his thoughts and doubts. He reflects on the vanity of it all, the seeming ultimate purposelessness of it. Yet, he never reflects on his thoughts themselves. He never reflects on his own inner moods and attitudes.

But thoughts, moods, and attitudes pass, vanish, return, combine, disappear—like the winds that Qoheleth notices so clearly. They are often all that we see, for we are claimed and gripped by them, held fast in the iron bars of the prison of this unending chatter.

"It is all hopeless," our thoughts sometimes flow. "Nothing ever works out for me." "Why am I the only one afflicted so? Why is everyone else fine, and I am filled with this inner turmoil?" "I hate those self-satisfied smug ones, filled with all sorts of good things, while I am filled only with anger and misery." Thoughts such as these, or others less intrusive—or others ten times worse—come and go constantly. Even when our thoughts are merely preoccupations about our to-do list, they are thoughts, and they preoccupy us and chain us fast to them.

Yet, it is possible to step back from these thoughts, to observe them, to notice them calmly without judging. It is possible just to be aware of them, possible just to "follow them" as the Desert Abbas and Ammas tell us, so as to learn about them. In doing so we become aware that there is more to us than just our thoughts, our moods, and our attitudes. There is something deeper, a substratum that lies beneath and beyond thoughts and moods, beyond our desires, conflict, doubt, and evanescence. We find we can be upheld by something deeper, a more fundamental state of simple awareness. And from this deeper place we notice our "inner chatter cannot cling to simple awareness. It simply appears and disappears in awareness like weather moving through the valley," says contemporary author Martin Laird.[1] Like the wind, like the weather, our thoughts and moods, both good and bad, come and go. Yet, there is a deeper place and presence within and beyond us. As we let the thoughts come and go, and pass beyond ourselves, this deeper place and presence can become the firm foundation of our lives. The seasons endure, the earth endures, sunrise and sunset endure, and so does our inner foundation, filled as it is with simple abiding awareness of all that is deeper, that is beyond the thoughts, that is a vast and stable spaciousness.

I remember that when I was a young adult, I was fascinated with my newfound awareness of God, the Church, and the allure of contemplative life. For several years, I thought that all of this was the truth, and yet I simply could not believe it. I tried to believe; I longed to believe. And I did believe—at least for a few days at a time! But quickly, inevitably, I would relapse into doubt. The external world would pull me back in, and I was quickly swallowed up in its mood of skepticism and rationalism, and in the quest for empirical evidence.

And then one day, when the longing for holiness came over me strongly, I irrevocably realized

my overwhelming need for God. No longer did I
think, "Well. Yes. *I* believe in you, God. *I* acknowl-
edge your existence." Instead, now I longingly
reached out for God. I had come to the end of my
ability to convince myself by means of thoughts. "I
need you, God," I said. "But I've come this route
before, and I can never hold on to faith. If I am to
truly believe, it can only happen if you hold on to
me."

And God did hold on to me. And so I was able
to believe, and trust, and move forward in my journey in faith. In some subliminal way, I'd realized
that thinking and thoughts wouldn't get me to
faith; it had to come from some deeper place, and
I'd allowed that deeper place to take root in me.

"The luminous simplicity of this grounding
awareness is beyond the reach of doubt,"[2] says
Laird, and I have experienced the truth of this.
Thoughts and moods, doubts and fears, all manner of difficulties and joys may come and go in our
lives, but this deeper center is beyond the reach of
their grasping, sucking vortices.

"Vanity of vanity, all is vanity," says Qoheleth,
and he is surely telling us truly about the constant
chatter of thoughts, impressions, and sensations
that pass through us in unending, relentless flow.
Life "passes swiftly, and we are gone," laments the
psalmist. This awareness can lead us to despair. It
can also teach us to turn our vision to something
deeper, to the calm inner spaciousness that is God's
abiding presence with us.

This perception of the frailty and mortality of
life can lead us to skepticism—or it can lead to a

deep perception of God's unchanging steadfast-
ness, perduring throughout the times and seasons
of humankind's brief span on earth.

> All people are grass,
> their constancy is like the flower of the field.
> The grass withers, the flower fades,
> when the breath of the Lord blows upon it;
> surely the people are grass.
> The grass withers, the flower fades;
> but the word of our God will stand forever. (Is 40:6–8)

This spacious awareness is always there—though
we aren't always aware of it! It is both reminder
and reality of God's steadfast love, unchanging
constancy, and constant availability to us.

The wisdom writers, of whom Qoheleth is
one, sought to find the unspoken rules for how to
conduct oneself in life. Following such rules, they
taught, would lead to the good life, a life blessed
right here on earth. Qoheleth follows this tradition,
but also questions it. "I know that whatever God
does endures forever," he writes. Yet, he also says,
"There is an evil that I have seen under the sun,
and it lies heavy upon humankind; those to whom
God gives wealth, possessions, and honor, so that
they lack nothing of all that they desire, yet God
does not enable them to enjoy these things, but a
stranger enjoys them. This is vanity; it is a grievous
ill" (Eccl 6:1–2).

All is vanity, Qoheleth says, all passes, and all
one can do is to live so as to distract oneself: "It is
fitting to eat and drink and find enjoyment in all
the toil with which one toils under the sun the few

days of the life God gives us; for this is our lot"
(Eccl 5:18).

Qoheleth, attributed to King Solomon, knew
only the wisdom of his time and his age. A later
time and a further revelation would take this wisdom deeper. Jesus said, speaking of himself, "something greater than Solomon is here" (Lk 11:31). Still
later Paul, pondering the mystery of God's revelation in Jesus the Christ, would say that Christ
is "the power of God and the wisdom of God" (1
Cor 1:24). For that same Jesus, through the scandal
of the Cross, reversed the normal human way of
apprehending wisdom. Because of Christ's death
and resurrection, because of the witness of the Spirit
in our hearts and lives, now we know that living a
good life, following the Lord, doesn't always mean
things will turn out well for us in this life. Now we
know that our ultimate vindication may wait until
after our "passover" into new and eternal life. Now
the wisdom has gone deeper. Now we know that
the blessed life in this world consists not in good
health, a good name, and possessions, but in the
availability of the Spirit in this blessed, gracious
awareness of God's abiding presence within.

And I, today, nearly forty years older than that
young adult who was held and nurtured in
faith through God's mercy, find myself continually pulled away to the life of externals. I need to
constantly work at returning to a deeper mode,

an unhurried rhythm, an awareness that moves underneath the constant chatter of thoughts and the clamor of desires, hopes, and doubts.

All is vanity, Qoheleth tells us, for it passes, much as wind and weather, sun and moon, springtime and winter, constantly change and pass. We cannot hold on to them. Yet, even so, all is gift in the simple awareness of the present moment. Both of these are valid; both of these are true. Like a March day, with its hint of spring and its echo of winter, we are called to live in both realities at one and the same time. They exist side by side, and the deeper wisdom enables us to live with them fruitfully. The book of Qoheleth is itself a *mashal*, a proverb. It leaves the contradictions intact, and thus "engage(s) the imagination by forcing it to press past the contradictions into the world of mystery," says scripture scholar Kathleen O'Connor.[3]

In March, huge drifts of dirty white snow lie alongside fields that have newly melted bare. The vernal equinox approaches. Darkness and light are briefly held in fragile, evanescent balance. The needles of the eastern white pine are old and yellow, getting ready to fall. Yet, the sap is rising in the deciduous trees, buds are swelling at the tips of branches, and maple sugaring season is here. The inner sap of simple awareness, divine wisdom, is always running in our hearts and in our veins. May we learn the sweetness of tapping into it.

spring

holy week

The sun is a warm caress on my back as I stoop over the raised flower bed. It is Palm Sunday, a quiet afternoon in early April. By some amazing miracle of weather, the snow has already disappeared. A tiny drift of it still remains in the corner of the cloister, where the sun almost never reaches. Even this is all but gone, melting rapidly in the mild temperature. The ground nearest the snow still shows a faint trace of wetness.

Here in the sunniest bed, farthest from the building, the snow vanished days ago, and the ground is soft and friable. Most years, it would be late April before I could get to this task, but now, after the toughest winter in nearly thirty years, spring has come early. The sun, the fresh air, the warmth—all are wonderful. My hands are filled with rabbit manure for the beds, and even this is wonderful! It may be Palm Sunday, it may only be the beginning of this week focused on Jesus' passion and death, but my spirit feels as if it's coming back to life.

The perennials are still barely stirring from their long winter's sleep. Only one or two show any signs of growth. Most are still bare and brown. Their roots are firmly attached to the cold earth, however, so I know they're still alive.

I stroll through the beds, checking on each of the plants. The lavenders, newly uncovered from their snowy mantle, are still greenish gray from last year. Those old leaves will turn dry and brown, but the new life is already coursing up through the stems; new growth is near at hand. Green tips of daylilies are bursting through the soil; two of the irises are showing growth. One sedum 'Autumn Joy' has new growth; the other, redder one is still holding back. A yarrow has feathery new wings of life. The primroses are planted nearer the building and have just lost their snow cover, so they aren't stirring yet. Out on the perimeter of the cultivated area, the daffodils are eight inches high. The southernwood shows no green, but when I try to break off the brown tops, the living stems refuse to snap. The bruised plant's fragrance is heady, a tantalizing reminder of summers past and summers still to come.

And the roses? I shake my head despairingly over them. I've never yet lost one of my English roses, even though they're marginal in this climate. But this winter might break my record. This winter might have been just too tough for them, no matter how deep their snowy insulation. The rugosas, however, those incredibly hardy species of roses, are already filled with green buds, well-nigh to leafing out.

I hadn't planned to work outside today, but the weather enticed me. This day is filled with a remarkable contrast—the warmth of the sun, the mild air, and yet a snowdrift lingers nearby. Under the top layer of soil, which is loose and easily worked, I can dig down into the cold, wet hardness of still frozen ground.

We have four huge raised beds here in the cloister garden, and I'm determined to work my way through one of them this afternoon. I'm busy scratching up the old mulch, taking out debris from last fall and the few weeds that have already been busy growing. I clean out a small patch, scratch up the mulch and scratch down into the soil, and then add rabbit manure. Even the manure heap has lost its snow and frost already. Wet and mucky it may be, at least in the middle, but it's usable.

"Black gold," I think, as I always do when working with manure, "black gold." Rabbit manure is even better black gold than just about any other kind. It was a gift from a neighbor late last November, and I could have put it straight on the garden, had I the time. Admittedly, though, it's more pleasant to wait until it's a little less fresh.

I shake the manure out of the bucket and use a hand tool, a small, three-pronged tilling fork, to work it into the soil. How good it is to be in the garden again, I think, musing on the importance

of gardens, which loom large in the scriptures. The
creation story in Genesis, where humanity first
began, took place in a garden. And its sequel, too,
the story of human downfall, took place in a garden; and humanity's punishment, in part, was ban-
ishment from the garden. Ezekiel, centuries later,
saw the restoration of Israel as an ever-growing
stream of flowing, fresh water, flowing from the
Temple, and giving birth to a garden of never-fail-
ing fruit along the banks. Jesus himself spent his
last night on earth in a garden and was handed
over to his enemies in a garden. "For you, who left
a garden, I was handed over . . . from a garden and
crucified in a garden" (Office of Readings for Holy
Saturday, Roman Breviary). According to John's
gospel, Jesus was buried and raised up again in
a garden. Here is a lesson, perhaps, that gardens,
however good in themselves, are only the setting
for human actions, and those actions can be good
or bad.

The garden, then, is a very appropriate place to
be for Holy Week. This week may be about suffering and death, but it is also about life. This corner of
the garden, on Palm Sunday afternoon, is a visible
witness to both: the warmth of sun and new life,
the persistent snowbank on its edge, and of course
the manure I am busily working into the soil.

I remember a course in spirituality I took a
long time ago. At one point the professor spoke
of the word "humility." "It comes from the Latin
word *humus,* meaning 'earth,'" she said. Even way
back then, I already knew that was only a partial
meaning. Humus is certainly earth, but any good

gardener knows it's not just any earth. It's not sand, which can't retain water. It's not clay, which retains entirely too much water. It's not even just ordinary topsoil, though that's a good start. Rather it's good, rich earth, filled with nutrients and organic matter. It comes from manure, or from compost, or from any kind of decaying organic material. The gift of humus is the best of all possible gifts for the garden. Fresh manure is good, but this already aged, already partly decayed manure is even better. It's already begun its transformation into humus.

Humility and humus, I reflect. Humility was that attitude toward life that completely filled Jesus; a total lack of arrogance. In Jesus, this meant a complete transparency, an utter fidelity to his Father's desire—a straightforward, unhesitating, uncompromising embrace of the truth. Jesus not only spoke the truth, but he lived the truth; he was and is the truth. "Humility is truth," said Teresa of Avila. This is not some sniveling, passive, defeatist, doormat approach to life. It is the truth of who we are, and who we are called to be.

Needless to say, we all too often aren't "simply who we are." We'd rather be anyone but ourselves! I know this is true for myself, certainly. I'd rather be—oh, just anyone else! Smarter, certainly, and funnier. When I was young I wished I were older! Then I wished to be more important and influential, too. Now I like to think of myself as calm, collected, and serene; organized and in charge of my destiny; yet open, docile to the Spirit, and always prayerful—someone who exudes an aroma of peace and holiness. Yes, that's who I am, right? Or at least, that's who I should be.

Or should I? Is it really such a good thing to allow myself these layers and layers of pretense? To hold on with all my strength to these spurious self-images? How does this relate to the person of Jesus, who emptied himself, who became truly human, one of us? How does this relate to the message of this week? And yet, who am I without these defenses?

Surely it's not good enough just to be the person I really am: often fearful, often worried, often irritable. Sometimes I seem to be filled with doubts and fears, rather than faith or peace. Often I am filled with uncertainty, too. Presumably I'm leading this little community, yet at the moment I don't know what our next step should be, or in which direction to aim it. All too often, indeed way too often, I'm a person who wants to tell the world: "Go away; leave me alone; make no more demands."

All of this is complicated by the fact that none of us, myself included, can just "be who we are" in public, at least not in the sense of letting our emotions hang out all over. There is polite and civil behavior, and appropriate behavior for each setting and relationship. The public face that we put upon our moods, emotions, and actions is in fact part of who we really are. But it isn't all of it, and it needs to relate in some consciously chosen way to our underlying state of being. To be truthful, it can't be a deliberate lie or a self-serving cover-up. We cover up our inner states often. To do so out of self-centeredness leads us away from truth and humility. To do so out of love only leads us deeper into truth.

Even when we can't let it all hang out publicly, we can always do so with God. And we should! To pretend or to lie to God, or to ourselves, means that we cut ourselves off from God. After all, God doesn't love or relate to the person I think I should be, or to the person I wish I was. God doesn't speak to the person I will be ten years down the road, or care about the person I was ten years ago, or even ten minutes ago. God isn't there for the perfect person I pretend to be. God loves, and relates to, and is always available to the person I actually am right here, right now. This very minute. So if I'm more interested in being someone else, somewhere else, I'll miss God entirely. I won't even be there for the God who is always right here for me.

Of course, we spend our lives learning to be who we really are. At least, we work at it. If we don't, we end up in old age a stranger to ourselves, and to God.

I think of a friend of mine, now seventy, who could not allow herself to admit the real reason for breaking off a seven-year friendship. Her good-bye letter didn't even give a reason. It was ostensibly filled with graciousness, but underneath I sensed anger. I think of this as I scratch manure into the garden. Her action caused so much anger, sadness, and hurt, a complicated roil of emotions I didn't know how to untangle for weeks. Today, the sun and warmth are so simple and soothing, but underneath, thick emotions flow. I am angry with her, and even more, I feel betrayed. Surely that's too strong a word. And yet, when a friend leaves without saying why, isn't that a betrayal? A betrayal of the basic honesty we all need in order to live out our days peacefully. Jesus certainly knew a betrayal far deeper than this, yet he went to meet it with peace and humility. Surely, with him as a model and guide, I can manage to do the same.

I think of the layers and layers of complex physical and chemical reactions going on in the soil, and in the decomposing manure. This is an apt image for the layers of dishonesty I feel in my friend's action, and the even greater layers of emotion it has generated within me. I powerfully feel this dishonesty, my friend's inability to speak the deeper truth. The profound reality of this broken relationship is like the elephant in the room that nobody can speak of. I know it's there, but it remains invisible and all the more present for being unseen and unwitnessed.

Jesus' death also had multiple realities. The official ones were presented by the powers that be, both Roman and Jewish. These were the stories of the rabble-rousing troublemaker, the revolutionary, the political force who had to be squelched. The Gospels give witness to the other reality. They witness to the unseen reality, which nearly everyone involved (including the disciples) wanted to ignore: the reality of the simple, humble, all too human God, who was so uncompromisingly truthful, and so uncompromisingly accepting of our own convoluted untruths. This Jesus "humbled himself and became obedient to the point of death—even death on a cross" (Phil 2:8); "he who, though he was in the form of God, did not regard equality with God as something to be exploited, but emptied himself, taking the form of a slave, being born in human likeness" (Phil 2:6–7).

Humility, and humus. Humility means allowing ourselves to deal with our own complications, our own truth, and our own untruth. Humility means accepting all the God-given gifts in our lives. It also means letting into our lives all the little deaths, all our own faults and failings. This is not complacency. Rather, it's a way of allowing ourselves to be very much less than perfect. In doing so, we nurture ourselves on the reality of our lives, and not on any false images of perfection. We can feed deeply on the reality that rises up out of the miseries, casualties, and complications of our daily lives, which amazingly brings new life out of this decaying and seemingly ruinous material. This reality is like humus, made of decomposing and disgusting matter, but which enlivens and enriches the garden.

The garden, like my life, has multiple realities. There is the sun, simple and warm and caressing on my back. There is the manure and the soil, complicated, grounding, messy, yet also ultimately life-giving. Both realities are part of who I am, who I was, who I will become. Humility means to be who I am, to embrace all of these realities. It means entering into the humility of Jesus. This humble and loving Lord fully embraced the human and divine reality of who he was. I am challenged to do the same.

fear,
my friend

I don't think I was actually born afraid. I think fear
came later. My earliest memories are sun-speckled,
golden, fearless. I remember playing in a wading
pool at a little friend's birthday party. Delighting
in a sundress. Running and screaming, heedless,
splashing in the pool and out, through the pool, the
water cool and delicious on my chubby little-girl
legs. With golden-white hair flying, water flying,
legs flying, it was exhausting and fun. No fear.

Eden, we pray, is granted in every child's life,
at least for a while. I guess it was in mine briefly,
though even early the shadows came crawling,
dark and fearful, reaching and grasping at childhood innocence. Thunderclouds mingled with sun
and water and golden drops of summer and playful
afternoons and flying hair, until memories fail and

I know not if I'm remembering sunshine or only pretending away the creeping, insidious, unassailable fears.

Yes, fear came early and came strong, and now I'm not sure if I actually experienced that little bit of Eden or if I only wished for it. Other Edens there were, later on in childhood: taking long, soothing walks in the woods when I was safely alone, or playing on the stone bridge over the brook in the lane on the way to the back lot of our farm. The bridge was made up of three huge, flat stones over the smooth, flowing dark water beneath, with large lady ferns and bracken brushing against the old Ford pickup as it jolted and rumbled across them when Pop drove out to the back lot to pick the late crop of sweet corn—the best of the season. The milky smell of the corn and the rough silkiness of the tassels contrasted with the dull, harsh heaviness of the heaped corn in its slatted wooden bushels.

Getting off the school bus on a lovely late September afternoon, I would find Mom cleaning and wiping tomatoes under the maple trees, and I joined her to help. The yellow jackets buzzed annoyingly at the broken, overripe tomatoes, but it was safe, oh safe, and the sun on the just-beginning-to-turn-color leaves was glorious. But then, years later, one day the sky turned a furious shade of green, and the wind picked up something fierce and blew the lawn chairs straight through the air. My brother grabbed the dog and got into the house before the tornado came down our road and uprooted both of those sugar maples, so lovingly planted by Mom decades before, and now no longer shading Mom and the tomatoes.

But I'm getting ahead of myself. The first day of school, with no warning, I found myself with about thirty other first graders walking down a stairwell that seemed to never end, and then down a dark long hall and into my first classroom. Mrs. Schlafer was stern and strict, and for two weeks I existed in her classroom in a kind of weary numbness, until in week three I was suddenly moved to Miss Costello's room, where the "bright" kids were and where everyone had a pastel-colored desk and many more crayons, and I seem to recall that most of us (and certainly I) could already print out our names and recite the alphabet. But they all knew each other before I got there, and I was scared, scared, scared and couldn't show it and naturally couldn't find a friend.

Here again I believe I learned safety. Safety came from being bright and knowing the answers.

Fear was fire at night and people out of control. Fear was Pop's temper, irritable at best, foreboding at worst. Fear was a summer with no rain and a farm drying up. Fear was the irrationality of life. Why did Pop, for one entire summer, sit outside under an oak tree at night and talk and talk and talk and gesticulate to himself, while I watched, fascinated and afraid, from a darkened upstairs window? Why were there unspoken rules and topics that were never mentioned? Why did Mom always speak of us as the "good" family, but others weren't? And if so, why did I somehow always know, without ever speaking it out, that I wasn't as good as anyone else? And so I was always afraid: afraid to comment or challenge or stand out in any way, except in terms of abysmal inferiority or absurdly posturing superiority.

And all to cover up, to cover up . . . what? To cover up the fears that metastasized until they consumed my inner life, which somehow still managed to survive in beauty, alone in the woods and fields, and which devoured books, immersed itself and drowned itself in them, if only to shut out the blackness of fear, the gnawing hopelessness, the overwhelming depth of worthlessness—because after all, I shouldn't be afraid, should I? Of course not, there was nothing to fear, was there?

So here I am, decades later, and still fearful. The fears have mutated over the years, but fear itself remains, permanently etched into my nervous system. As a child and young adult, the fears—at least those I acknowledged—were social: Will other people like me? Will I be accepted? As responsibilities increased and my vocation developed, the fears changed to match the changing situation. But always, way deep down, remained an unspoken fear, a capital fear. As a child, I came close to death on more than one occasion. Always I was helpless. Always I panicked. Anxiety, a vast fog overwhelming my brain, blotted out all, but the fear lived on, unacknowledged, subterranean. The more powerful therefore, it fed all the other fears. Today it can still spring up into daylight, evoked by an event in my daily life. Fire, for instance, always has the power to terrify me.

Consider this: a bright, windy day in early May. The snow is long gone, the grass is beginning to grow, but leaves and underbrush are still brown and dry, tinder dry. I am working in the perennial border, digging compost into the soil. Suddenly I hear hissing and crackling. The cat, who has been out prowling for mice, comes on a run and flings himself at the door to be let inside. I realize there's a brush fire somewhere close by, and it's probably out of control. Anxiety surges and nearly overwhelms my brain. My legs and arms seem numb. I head toward the sound of fire, trying to run, but there's no adrenalin rush; instead my feet feel like lead, and I go slower and slower, barely able to push myself forward. I am drowning with panic.

Finally I arrive at the fire. A neighbor has been burning over his field, and it got away into ours. I shout to him to ask if I should call the fire department. He responds angrily. "It's under control," he snarls. "Get out of here; get away." I wait until there is no immediate danger. My panic slowly subsides, and I stand my ground, watching until I'm sure it is fully controlled, and then I slowly turn away.

"Adam died because he sinned; we sin because we die." So runs a pithy saying in the Orthodox Church. The fear of death in so many ways rules

our lives. Fight or flight are two extremes of the
instinctive response to threat and danger. The ultimate threat, the ultimate danger, is annihilation. In
Eden, presumably, there was no threat or danger.
But our first parents turned away from God and
were banished from Eden into the world of death.
"Adam died because he sinned." For all of us the
fear of death or annihilation lurks deep down at the
heart of all our fears, and of fear-driven behavior.
"We sin because we die." For those growing up
in fear laden families, fear is not something that
rears its frightful head only occasionally. Fear is an
ever-present menace, a shadow that accompanies
us everywhere and at all times.

"We sin because we die." I have no doubt that
death is at the heart of fear, though it cleverly dis-
guises itself with many masks. The social fears of
a teenager and young adult unprepared for coping
with adult life and relationships slowly morphed
into deeper, more dire fears as I grew into my life
vocation and moved away from mainstream contemplative life into the rocky road of a calling to
solitude. I felt so different and unique. I feared
being seen as different. Paradoxically I also feared
being invisible. The inner journey became everything, its outer clothing drab and deceptive. I hated
the dreaded question, "And what do you do?" and
the task of explaining a life of solitude. At the same
time, I bitterly resented the invisibility of the hermit
life to those who remained safe and secure in highly
esteemed contemplative communities. Either way
felt like facing death: a death due to neglect or dis-
belief or a death due to overestimation.

Moving off the grid of religious life meant also moving off the grid of mainstream American economic life. I desperately feared financial and social annihilation. This anxiety was outrageously overdeveloped, but at the time it was real enough. Indeed all fears are "real enough" at the time, to the one who is fearful. I learned gradually to see them in perspective. My dread alerted me to the presence of real concerns and the need to take preventive action. But they were only part of my life, not the whole of it. They were fears and nothing more.

As my journey continues, I find that my terrors have changed and developed with me. Now that I approach my elder years, I fear the diminishment of aging. My body once seemed invincible. Now it continually tugs at my consciousness with aches and pains. I fear the helplessness and vulnerability of aging, and even more, I fear I will be unable to accomplish all that I hope to do in life.

"Why are you afraid?" Jesus asks his disciples in the midst of a powerful storm (Mk 4:40). "What a foolish question," we might be tempted to think. How could they not be afraid? How can anyone not be afraid in the midst of the storms of life? Yet, we are asked to move beyond fear into trust. How easy it is, in the midst of danger, crisis, and storm to let fear overpower us, until all we are is one great, quaking mass of fear. In speaking out our fears and identifying them, we become empowered. We find an island, an oasis, a tiny piece of inner ground that is beyond the fear. We remember that we are more than just fear, and so we are enabled to take the first step in moving beyond fear onto the solid ground of trust and hope. As a child I fled from fear, and it pursued me everywhere. I sought safety as an antidote and believed that reason and control would keep fear at bay. But fear was stronger.

Jesus asks a second question of his disciples: "Have you still no faith?" (Mk 4:40). That very day they had seen his powerful deeds and heard his teachings of the kingdom. But they were overtaken by their fears. And so am I, time after time. So are we all.

At bottom, all our fears are about some sort of death: our physical death or any of the multitude of smaller deaths that fill our days and haunt our nights. In the midst of life I have feared death many times: as a child, as a young adult, in middle age, and now as I begin my later life. Death takes many forms and faces, as do the corresponding fears. What is constant is the fact of fear, undulating in and out of my days and accompanying me with its chill presence. Faith never permanently banishes it, no matter how I try.

Slowly over the years I have come to realize that fear is God's emissary, my true friend. It is not a fair-weather friend; rather, it challenges, confronts, and provokes me, facing me down, twisting in my belly.

It demands attention, yet under its stern façade it seeks an attentive ear and a heart filled with deep and respectful listening. It seeks befriending. Its presence reminds me to return to myself and listen deeply to what drives my fears. How easily I forget, in the busyness and distractions of the day, that this life is not everything; how easily I forget a deeper awareness and presence—until fear nudges up against me, blossoming in my heart and mind and gut, twisting me, calling attention to itself and to whatever I dread. This can lead to the unraveling of faith, but it can also return me to the memory of God and God's strengthening and peaceful presence. Fear is God's angel, a true messenger, a reminder of the limitations of life and the greater horizons of God's loving mercy. My terrors challenge me to broaden my horizons and deepen my perspective.

seeds of wisdom

This year we're breaking new ground for the vegetable garden. The garden will be much closer to the building, and far more convenient and manageable. But it's a long, hard process. Today I am picking rocks and weeds from the garden. Last June we had trees taken out and the stumps removed. Now, the soil is uneven. Where stumps and roots were rudely wrenched out last summer, the underground tunnels made by the loss of the roots have collapsed over winter, leaving a rutted, bumpy surface. Planting is hard work on this new ground, with lots of small sticks, rocks, and pieces of sod to remove.

As I place seeds, one after another, in a row that will someday bring us the pleasure of fresh peas, I marvel at the destruction this patch of earth

went through, and the transformation that has
been wrought in it. Huge equipment came and cut
down the trees right at the earth, shredded them
into wood chips, and took the chips away. More
huge, noisy equipment came and tore the roots out
of the ground and took them away, too. The trees,
the grass, the earth itself—all were helpless before
the onslaught of equipment, brought about by the
desire of human beings to make a garden where
once there were trees. The earth was laid bare and
empty, made ready to be transformed.

Planting a garden is a great exercise in faith at
the best of times: we prepare the soil, plant, water,
fertilize, mulch, weed—and hope for the best. Last
year we had nonstop rain and damp weather in
June, July, and much of August. It was the worst
gardening year ever, demonstrating plainly that so
much of gardening is utterly beyond our control.
We do our best with what we can, and leave the
remainder to God's unfathomable mercy. Modern
science, agricultural practices, and even the folk
wisdom handed down over generations can often
only attempt to mitigate the devastation caused by
weather, disease, bugs, and critters large and small.

Even the ever-moving seasons are a reminder
of the fragility of the moment, the changeableness
of the weather, and the instability of our fortune.
"To everything there is a season," says Ecclesiastes
(3:1), and the unspoken corollary is that the seasons
keep moving. The '60s song that brought this to
life added "turn, turn, turn." Good fortune does
not last, nor does summer. Summer becomes fall
becomes winter becomes spring becomes summer

again. The turning of the seasons gives us both death and new life. The passing days and years can equally bring destruction to human life or can bring renewal.

I think of the miners in West Virginia and Kentucky, working in tunnels thousands and thousands of feet underground. Their tunnels collapsed, and they died, as surely as our trees. I think of the trees, growing to their prime, only to be cut and killed, because they were in the wrong place. How like the miners, or so many others: victims of accidents, terrorists, earthquakes, hurricanes, or other unexpected disasters. Death, injury, and destruction can come so suddenly and without warning.

Equally unexpected, sometimes we are surprised by grace. A friend visits us, the beauty of a sparkling new day infects us with joy, a fortunate windfall is given us. "A generous measure, pressed down, shaken together, running over, will be poured into your lap" (Lk 6:38). The positive, joyous events usually evoke no questions from us. We don't complain or argue or ask why. Like children on their birthdays, we are only too ready to welcome all the good things life brings. All too often, we assume they are our due.

But the hard things—oh, what a different story! How I hate to see the nights lengthening, the days growing short. How I grumble at shoveling snow! How I complain about cold days and nights, about the length and dreariness of interminable winter. How angry and impatient I become when things don't go my way. How keenly I feel the pain of grief, hurt, and suffering. Indeed, what a different story.

Injury, destruction, and the death of his loved ones came for Job suddenly and without warning. With its unfolding drama and dialogues, the book of Job can be seen as an extended meditation on the question of why the innocent suffer. How does one cope with such horrible happenings? What possible answers can there be? What wisdom can enable one to endure such pain?

Suffering spills over in Job as he curses the injuries he has suffered. His three friends, Eliphaz, Bildad, and Zophar, try to comfort him with conventional responses. Surely you have done something wrong, Job, and these tragedies are the recompense for your sins! Admit your fault; humble yourself; bear witness to the truth! Job, however, persists in his stubborn innocence. He will not admit to being at fault, he will not humble himself, and he insists that God must answer him.

> But I would speak to the Almighty,
> and I desire to argue my case with God.
> As for you, you whitewash with lies;
> all of you are worthless physicians.
> If only you would keep silent,
> that would be your wisdom! (Jb 13:3–5)

Job's insistence on innocence rubs us the wrong way. No human being is ever innocent, we think. Children, perhaps. But adults? How easily we think that victims did something to deserve their fate, or at least to bring it on themselves. "She shouldn't have walked there late at night," we say of a rape victim. Or, "He shouldn't have built his house by the ocean. He knew the danger from hurricanes." When tragedy befalls us, we list again, over and over, the things we should have done differently, the reasons why we brought this on ourselves. Worse, we believe that God must be punishing us. "I've done something awful," we think. "God must be penalizing me for it." And so Job's protestations of innocence fall on deaf ears. Like his three friends, we offer ourselves false consolations; we take blame and guilt on ourselves—or heap it on the backs of those we deem acceptable scapegoats.

To step back from tragedy, to attempt some sort of perspective, we try to ask the same questions in a less personal way. Where is wisdom in all this? How do I handle the devastation of tragedy in an upright way? How do I allow myself not to become trapped in my grief, guilt, and loss?

In chapter 28, the writer of Job has also inserted a more philosophical, less intensely personal reiteration of these persistent themes: Where is wisdom to be found? How can I find meaning in seemingly senseless tragedy?

At first, it seems hopeless. Even as miners carve trackless paths beneath the earth's surface, or birds of prey soar the trackless paths of the sky, the writer cautions us that the path to wisdom is equally unknown. "Where then does wisdom come from? And where is the place of understanding? It is hidden from the eyes of all living, and concealed from the birds of the air" (Jb 28:20–21). But as this chapter of Job progresses, the tone changes. The writer comes to terms with the incomprehensibility

of God's ways, and discovers anew the unvary-
ing response about wisdom: "God understands
the way to it, and he knows its place. And he said
to humankind, 'Truly, the fear of the Lord, that is
wisdom; and to depart from evil is understanding'
(Jb 28:23, 28)."

The fear of the Lord, that is wisdom. This classic
response of the Hebrew wisdom tradition, developed and augmented over the course of centuries,
always remained its heart. Those who wrote in wisdom's school taught that by the fear of the Lord and
the carrying out of the commandments, one could
lead a good, even a blessed life. The opening song
of the Psalter, a wisdom psalm, tells us, "Happy are
those who do not follow the advice of the wicked.
. . . They are like trees . . . which yield their fruit in
its season, and their leaves do not wither. In all that
they do, they prosper" (Ps 1:1, 3). Proverbs, Sirach,
Wisdom, and numerous psalms all convey a similar
message. Do good, follow God's commandments
and laws, and all will be well with you.

Yet, obviously, doubts remained, for included
in the wisdom writings are Job, who struggles
because he suffers in spite of having lived a good
life; and Ecclesiastes, that profound skeptic who
sees that both good and bad happen equally.

Job's dilemma, and that of the wisdom writers,
is that the evidence is clear that all too often bad
things do indeed happen to good people. No one
has ever explained this satisfactorily, though people have tried for millennia. Jesus experienced this
to the full: he was rejected, condemned, suffered,
and died. Yet, we believe that he is the only one of

the entire human race who is in himself perfectly good, perfectly innocent. Recent studies reveal that the authors of the gospels portray him as a wisdom figure. This gives us an astounding insight into the early Christian reworking of the wisdom tradition—and into Jesus. The fear of the Lord, the following of the laws and commandments, does indeed still lead to the blessed life; yet, this good life is not inconsistent with the most horrendous suffering. Perhaps Job had an advance preview of this, for in the end, he is reconciled to his fate—and his questions—by God himself. (Though an unknown editor added an ending that "he lived happily ever after, and all his wealth and good fortune was restored to him." I notice that the introduction to Job—where Satan asks God's permission to test Job—and the end are in prose, while the wonderful body of the book, where all the weighty questions are asked and ultimately both answered and unanswered, is in poetry.)

In retrospect we can see that Job, in his innocence and his suffering, is a type, a symbol, a figure, for the Christ. We see, through the swirling shadows of time, that earlier wise ones were grappling with how to reconcile wisdom and suffering. Not that there was any conscious inkling of the Jesus that God had in store for the human race. But a sketchy outline is there: in stubbornly sticking to his innocence, Job elicits a personal response from the Most High. It leaves him gasping, head over heels in his own estimation, but how could any interaction with the Almighty be otherwise?

This overturning of the foundations of Job's thoughts and questions becomes the pattern for the disciples' response to Jesus. "Blessed are the poor. Blessed are those who mourn. Blessed are the peacemakers. Blessed are those persecuted . . ." (see Mt 5:3–13). The Beatitudes leave us gasping as well. Surely he can't mean them literally! Blessed means happy. How similar, and yet how unimaginably greater.

"For since, in the wisdom of God, the world did not know God through wisdom, God decided, through the foolishness of our proclamation, to save those who believe" (1 Cor 1:21). "We proclaim Christ crucified . . . Christ the power of God and the wisdom of God. For God's foolishness is wiser than human wisdom, and God's weakness is stronger than human strength" (1 Cor 1:23, 24–25). The wisdom teacher Jesus is instructing us in the paths of God's wisdom. Jesus-Wisdom builds on human wisdom, and then transforms it. Yes, we are called to fear of the Lord, to keep the commandments and laws. "Do not think that I have come to abolish the law or the prophets; I have come not to abolish but to fulfill" (Mt 5:17). Yet, this same discourse begins with the Beatitudes and continues with Jesus-Wisdom reiterating, "You have heard it said to you, but I say to you . . ." Keeping the commandments is only the beginning; there is more to wisdom than that. He ends with the story of the two men, one who built his house on sand, the other on rock. The rock on which to build, of course, is no longer the following of the commandments, not even the Torah, but the following of Jesus and

Jesus-Wisdom's way and commands. This is truly the way to the good, the blessed, the unshakeable life, built on the rock who is the Messiah, the Savior. This wisdom-way will see us through any storm, even that of unspeakable, devastating suffering. It builds not on our own innocence or good works, but on the saving actions and constant presence of the ultimate innocent, Jesus.

Beyond the person of Jesus, stretching through the centuries, Christian monasticism is also a wisdom tradition. As Benedict tells us in the preface to the *Rule,* the monastery is a "school for the Lord's service." Like the wisdom schools run by the sages of Israel, the *Rule* sets out the guidelines for wise living. It exposes our daily experience to the loving scrutiny of the new law of love expounded by the true sage, Jesus. The wisdom of the *Rule,* as of the entire monastic tradition, is gently teaching us how to live our daily lives so as to be blessed, to be happy. It teaches not merely the intellect, but the whole person. The monastic educators are not only the abbot, but the entire community. We are taught not only through the written word, but by immersion in monastic life itself. Wisdom is learned primarily by the heart, not the head. Through our heart we learn to discern the voice of the Spirit, speaking in the events and relationships of our daily lives. As stated in the title of Joan Chittister's book on Benedict's *Rule,* "wisdom [is] distilled from the daily."

The day-to-day of ordinary life overtakes all of us as adults. Life gets busy, we get busy, and then, unfortunately, tragedy and suffering strikes.

What monasticism offers is the unending discipline of learning to step back, to take time to pray and ponder the scriptures—the discipline to talk to and learn from Jesus-Wisdom. Such wisdom can be learned at all times and in all situations, but we must work at it.

What are some of the things this ancient tradition of wisdom teaches us? From Job, we hear that we should talk to God and be very honest about ourselves. Do not pretend to accept the established way of looking at our situation. Do not conform to what we know to be false. True fear of the Lord implies honesty and integrity. If we are inwardly raging at God, do not deny it. God can handle our rage. God will respect it. Talk to God out of the depths of where we truly are.

In Jesus, we see wisdom teaching and preaching, healing and feeding, and avoiding the verbal traps set by his enemies. More than this, the wisdom of Jesus is shown forth also when he often takes time out to pray. He does this when he needs respite from the multitudes, or before important decisions, and especially before he faces condemnation, torture, and death. In the portrait of Jesus in Gethsemane we see a close-up of Jesus at prayer. He, too, speaks to God. He begs his Father for help, begs that his fate may be different. In doing so, like Job, he speaks out of his integrity. But his integrity goes further, for it embraces what is and accepts what cannot be changed.

In the Gospel of Luke, we see Jesus talking to his Father in Gethsemane, and also listening. He is attentive to his situation and to what God is speaking in his heart. He asks for help, and he receives it, not in the way he'd hoped—"Father, please take this cup away from me"—but in the strength to bear it: the angels came and ministered to him (see Lk 22:42–43). Like Job, Jesus-Wisdom speaks out of his integrity to his Father. But he also deeply listens and opens himself to what he hears. Jesus-Wisdom knows how to listen to and interpret God's silence, and he models this attentive listening to all of us.

St. Benedict has learned deeply in this school of wisdom, and he shares his insight with us in his *Rule*. Pray often, he says. Talk to God. Speak to him through the psalms, and in your own words as well, "with tears, and compunction of heart."[1] Most of all, listen!

God is speaking to us all the time, Benedict says, even in the most catastrophic events. Jesus says this also, in his words and with his life. The entire wisdom tradition reminds us that in all that happens, in all whom we meet, in the deepest movements of the heart, God is present. Everything is a seed of wisdom. If we cultivate these seeds daily, we will reap a rich harvest. We sow them in the good soil of integrity by being true to who we are and how we feel. We water them with daily doses of attentiveness, and fertilize them with prayer. In the warm sunshine of a listening heart, they will mature and bear fruit a hundredfold.

Catastrophe strikes each of us at some time in our lives. When this happens, each one of us is in some way Job. We are each of us, in some way, Jesus as well. And yet, we are each of us ourselves—unique and irreplaceable. Seeds of wisdom tell us that Job's story is Christ's story is the trees story is the miners' story is the oil-spill story is the world's story is my story. Seeds of wisdom, sown in our hearts, remind us that in bad times as well as good, we are never alone.

gifts of the spirit

The first of the rugosa roses opened in time for Vespers of the Vigil of Pentecost. The weather had been cold and wet for three days, but on Saturday it began to warm, and by early afternoon, the sun broke through. Warm and muggy, the air brooded, building up to a thunderstorm, and sure enough the rain returned at just about Vespers time. Before it came, however, there was enough warmth to coax one red rosebud into opening.

Early Pentecost morning, I woke to a delightful world with swirls of fog, mist, and sunlight. As the morning progressed, the fog dissipated, and the day was clear, bright, and warm. More thunderstorms were predicted, the leading edge of a cold front marching in from the west. Before they arrived, several more rugosas opened, and the crinkled green leaves of the shrubs shone dark in contrast to the clear rose of the newly opened flowers.

Pentecostal flowers are normal around here, but each year they are new and enchanting. From mid-May until mid-June, Maine is inundated with spring flowers, especially flowering trees. The lilacs are in full bloom now, breathing their fragrance into every breeze, a feast to my senses of sight and smell and touch. Honeysuckle is also in bloom, and the ubiquitous autumn olive; these, too, are immensely fragrant. The blueberries are coming to the end of blossom time, but the brambles, both wild and cultivated, are just opening their simple, five-petaled white flowers.

Daffodils are long gone, decayed into senescence until next year, and tulips have faded. In the outer field, an early daylily has opened, yellow and rust; and at the stone-wall garden, culinary sage and valerian sport large, full heads. The purple heads of the chives attract huge reddish-gold bumblebees.

And everywhere, there is green: the green of fields ready for haying, the green of lawns and gardens, the multihued greens of leaves on the trees. The leaves are still young and tender, with a softer look than the mature leaves of summer.

The power and lush richness of all this new life is a recurring yearly miracle. This year it all coincides with Pentecost. So often, I think of Easter or Christmas when I think of the gift of new life. This year, I am reminded that all life is a gift of the Spirit, which is given to us in such rich abundance at Pentecost. Every year from Ascension Thursday to Pentecost, we enter into that great nine days of prayer during which we await the renewed out-pouring of the Spirit. This tradition first began with Mary and the disciples as they gathered in one place to pray and wait for the Spirit, the great-est gift from the One who bestows all good gifts.

Spring is always the time of Pentecost, and on at least two occasions, an extraordinarily lovely spring became the container, the lovely outer cov-ering, for a special gift. The first time was the day in May when I became Catholic, a day I had been longing and praying for. I was so young and new to my faith, but I had learned of the gifts of the Spirit. Because this was to be a very special day for me, I prayed for a special grace from the Spirit. I wanted the gift of prayer.

Even then I suspected this might be an unusual gift. Very early in the Church, St. Paul wrote: "There are varieties of gifts, but the same Spirit. To one is given through the Spirit the utterance of wisdom, and to another the utterance of knowledge accord-ing to the same Spirit, to another faith by the same Spirit, to another gifts of healing by the one Spirit, to another the working of miracles, to another prophecy, to another the discernment of spirits, to another various kinds of tongues, to another the interpretation of tongues. All of these are activated by one and the same Spirit, who allots to each one individually just as the Spirit chooses" (1 Cor 12:4, 8–11).

As the centuries rolled on, traditional Catholic spirituality began to define these gifts of the Spirit as sevenfold: wisdom, understanding, counsel, fortitude, knowledge, piety, and fear of the Lord. Then there are also the fruits of the Spirit: "The fruit of the Spirit is love, joy, peace, patience, kindness, generosity, faithfulness, gentleness, and self-control" (Gal 5:22–23). All of these are wonderful gifts, superb qualities that help us live out our lives in a good and upright and healthy manner. But I was stuck on what I wanted: the gift of prayer—not a gift mentioned in the scriptures, not even on the Church's list of Spirit-given gifts, yet representing what seemed to be my heart's desire.

That Pentecost Sunday came and went, a lovely day, filled with spring and with the Spirit. Communion was only given on the tongue back then, and I had never considered the logistics of actually receiving it. The priest had to whisper to me, "Stick out your tongue." It was a private Mass, held at the little convent around the corner from the church. The sisters had prepared a small reception, and afterward I left with a friend for the drive back to Connecticut.

The gift of prayer? I never realized at the time how deeply it was given. All I knew then was peace, the most profound peace of my entire young life. Twenty-two years old, I had never known till then what true peace was like. I had no idea of the depth of this blessing. On the drive home, my friend chattered away happily, but I could only nod and smile. I was sublimely preoccupied, entranced, held captive by the profound depth of this sudden and immense interior peace. There was inner chattering, no thoughts chasing themselves busily

around my mind, no interior dialogues, no manifestations of inner compulsions—just peace, and
freedom, and immense spaciousness.

"When the sea [of the mind] is calm, fisher-
men perceive the movement of its depths. . . . To
the Holy Spirit alone does it belong to purify the
spirit" (Diadochus of Photike, Office of Readings
for Wednesday of Week 4, Roman Breviary).

That night, as I was staying over with friends,
a vase of flowers I'd brought back with me was on
the nightstand. Several times that night I awoke
briefly to moonlight in the room, on the flowers,
and to their fragrance—and to peace, always peace,
the most profound depths of peace.

The next day arrived, and then the next, and
the next after that. Life went on, and so did I. Peace
continued, with greater or lesser awareness, for
several weeks. Gradually it faded, and gradually
the real world returned over the course of these
weeks. I was too young and too inexperienced in
the ways of the Spirit to understand what had happened. I knew only that it was wonderful, beyond
my experience, and utterly fulfilling.

That was many years ago, yet the remembrance
of that peace has never left. Often there are tantalizing reminders of it, like wisps of fog, floating and
blowing through mind and heart, reminding me of
the depths that hover close by, awaiting a chance
to seep into awareness. Over the years I've also
learned that such profound peace can only be the
gift of the Spirit, and that it is indeed prayer. I've
learned that prayer is about relationship, not just
about words. It's about attention, and awareness

of God. It's about awareness of ourselves, too, and it's about the long, ceaseless struggle to find our way through our own tangles, compulsions, and convolutions, into the depths of our hearts where God dwells. To open myself to the gift of prayer means to open myself to relationship and to intimacy—with God, surely, but also with myself. Knowledge of God comes only with knowledge of self. "May I know you, may I know myself," said St. Augustine.[1] As a recent writer said, Augustine was "an exemplar of the search through human experience as the surest path to sacred illumination."[2] Indeed, God "communicates with us through our own inner truth," says Merton.[3]

The years since then have been filled with blessings and also with struggles. Even as I began to appreciate the immensity of the gift I was given on my first Pentecost, I've also slowly come to understand and accept the many intricate layers that have kept my heart from being open and from receiving this gift more often. The long journey of life is a struggle, but it has had intention and meaning. My heart, the place of God's dwelling, has gradually become at least a bit more accessible.

Just before this Pentecost I was blessed with yet another grace, a visit to the shrine of St. Anne de Beaupré in Quebec. It's a relatively easy drive from Maine, and I'd never visited it. So for the first time in my monastic life, I went on a pilgrimage. Just myself and another sister, it was a brief visit for quiet and prayer. I was not expecting much of anything, I was even afraid that I'd be left cold and unmoved by this immense church and this very traditional devotion.

It was yet another beguiling day in this supremely enticing spring. We had a beautiful drive, up through northwestern Maine and into Canada. We managed to get lost twice in Quebec City, but otherwise it was uneventful. As we approached the town of St. Anne de Beaupré, we could see the enormous church, a basilica, from far away. "That must be it," I said to Sr. Bernadette, and sure enough, it was. We visited at the end of the off-season when the shrine's own inn was not yet open, so we put up in a nearby motel. We checked in, freshened up, unpacked, and made a stop for a bowl of soup at the restaurant next-door.

At a little after six on a captivating spring evening, we walked over to the shrine. The huge bronze doors stood hospitably open to the mild air. We walked through the foyer, and into the nave, and immediately we were confronted with two enormous pillars, rising at least forty feet high, and covered with crutches: the wordless testimonies, the artifacts of healings.

Before and above us stretched the immense space of the basilica. We were completely alone in it. We walked around slowly, immersed in the vast, loving silence. At some point we separated, each cocooned in stillness. I paused at the side altars, and at the mementos of all the Canadian dioceses. I stopped at the magnificent main altar, with its soaring gold baldachin, and stopped again at the majestic and regal tabernacle.

Most of all, the blessed weight of hundreds of years and millions and millions of heart-wrenching prayers stilled and filled me. I sank into the depth of it. Finally I reached the lovely statue of St. Anne, and her altar. I knelt to pray. To my astonishment, I burst into tears. My heart opened, and I heard myself saying, "I never had a grandmother!" I sobbed and sobbed and sobbed, and over and over my heart repeated soundlessly, "I never had a grandmother, I never had a grandmother, I never had a grandmother."

It was true. My grandparents had all died long before I was born. I never even missed them, never gave them a thought. How could I? I never had an inkling of what I was missing. Yet, somehow my heart, that place made for God and God's infinite embracing love, knew its loss, and named it grandmother.

Minutes passed, then more minutes, and then still more. Still I wept, and still I lamented the loss of the grandmother I had never known. My heart, which moments before had only lightly embraced the beauty of the spring evening and the satisfaction of a safe arrival, was pierced with awareness of its own loss, sorrow, misery, and hopelessness. There was no grandmother, with her all-embracing, unconditional love. There never would be. I was encompassed in misery. Like a child who knows only this moment, and no before or after, misery and hopelessness was all there was. The quintessence of all the negativity I'd ever encountered in all my early years enveloped me. I was lost in it. Endurance was the only positive response I knew.

Misery, and loss, and hopelessness: this is what had always filled my heart. Despair that it could ever be different. How could I have ever failed to see this before? How could I have hidden it so well from myself?

Gradually, I pulled myself up and away, though I was still numb and dead inside. The outside world returned. The evening passed, and the night. The next morning, at Mass, the loss returned, though not so strongly. Throughout the day it continued to recur, and again in the days that followed. I mused again and again, reflecting on it, and realizing again, from within the experience, the immensity of loss and grief. Surely, I thought, this is who I am at rock bottom, just an experience of loss and emptiness. Surely I had known this; and yet, I didn't—not really.

"To know God, to know ourselves." Though I have spent many years getting to know myself, and though I had experienced glimpses of these feelings before, this was surely the most profound experience I ever had of the depths of my own heart. Throughout the past several months I had felt I was standing outside my heart, knocking, unable to enter. Suddenly, unexpectedly, my heart had opened, and I was standing within. Yet, this place within was revealed as a place of utmost desolation! At least now I felt connected to myself, I thought, even though it is such a place of grief and misery. At least I am *chez moi*, at home with myself. Better to be within, even in misery, than to be in "the outer darkness, where there will be weeping and gnashing of teeth" (Mt 8:12).

Time went on, we returned home, and Ascension and the days leading up to Pentecost arrived. By now this profound awareness of loss and grief had lost its edge. It was still present, but more in memory than current experience. It was so profound, however, that I kept reflecting on it, my thoughts ever circling round it. On Ascension Thursday I had again been reflecting on it during prayer, in conjunction with one of the readings for the day: "You will receive power when the Holy Spirit has come upon you" (Acts 1:8). I began to reflect that perhaps I, too, had received empowerment from the Spirit. Perhaps I did not need to sit in grief and loss and hopelessness forever. Perhaps I had a choice: the choice of sitting in my hopelessness, or of chosing hope. Not a once and forever choice, it was a choice to make, and remake and make again, over and over, each and every day. It was a choice with no guarantees that I would be able to move out of my hopelessness, other than the guarantee in faith that at least there is the possibility.

Pentecost arrived, and spring continued, with all its attendant garden work. I was busy with gardens, and writing, and preparing for construction of the retreat house, and fundraising, and Oblates, and a multitude of things. In the midst of it, I forgot about hopelessness, and desire for a grandmother, and gifts of the Spirit. I forgot totally, until one day at prayer, as I cast my gaze inward, I realized that hopelessness was gone; gone was the dark funk of the last several months; gone was the misery, the grief, the loss.

Yet, I was still connected, somehow, in some degree, to living from my heart. I thought of St. Anne, and I thought, "my grandmother." In hindsight, I can see that all that grief and loss and hopelessness was held, contained, and embraced in the warmth and love of a grandmother's loving heart.

It all began with the gift of that first Pentecost, the gift of peace, when for the first time I experienced God's loving embrace. Ever since, even though I've been mostly unaware, God has been holding and containing and embracing me in love and peace. Mostly this has been unseen, unfelt. But still God's presence has always been there. Like the silent, prayer-permeated openness of St. Anne's basilica, this unseen, loving presence of God has been the blessed container that enabled me to know and accept myself.

What happened at St. Anne's? What brought up this knowledge of my heart? No doubt it was the blessed stillness and spaciousness, which allowed my heart to surrender its wound. What enabled me to perceive and understand? It was all the years of working to find and live from my heart. Finally, what healed it? It could only be the loving, grandmotherly embrace of God.

Gifts of the Spirit, gifts of prayer: they happen in strange and wonderful and always loving ways, often when we least expect. My early desire for prayer, and the totally unexpected revelation of early loss, emptiness, and helplessness: these are gifts of the Spirit, given in God's own time and way. Only God knows the when and why. We can only open our hearts to receive the grace.

I know only this. If you ask me now if I have a grandmother, I will answer yes.

summer

ordinary time

The Church's year and the garden's year don't always coincide, at least not in Maine. Pentecost usually falls on a Sunday in late May or early June. After Pentecost, the Church resumes what it calls Ordinary Time. But in a Maine garden, this is still the time of planting seeds and setting out seedlings, that time when all the growing things are first bursting into exuberant new life. The last frost occurs in mid- to late May, and only after frost can many of the young vegetables or annuals go out to their permanent homes in the soil. There's nothing ordinary about it: it's the extraordinary time when everything is urgent, and it all needs to be done, at once, *now!*

But as June continues, and the garden settles in for the summer, it, too, becomes ordinary.

There's still mulching and weeding and watering, and later there will be picking and deadheading, as well as dividing and moving a few perennials. But these are all just the everyday tasks of ordinary, typical summer. The perennials begin their usual succession of bloom, the veggies and fruits their succession of ripening. It's normal and ordinary, sometimes even a bit boring. True, there are spectacular moments: when the roses are all in bloom, or the Oriental lilies first open, or when the first peaches or melons ripen. But mostly, day after day, it's all the same.

What do we mean when we say "ordinary"? The dictionary defines it as "of the usual kind, not exceptional." But this is a definition only by way of negation. In the liturgical year, Ordinary Time refers to all the time not covered by particular Church seasons such as Advent, Christmas, Lent, or Eastertide.

Most of us think of ourselves as ordinary people—there's nothing exceptional about us. We're not glamorous rock stars or film stars or major politicians. We're not investment bankers or entrepreneurs. We're not sports stars, and we probably are not counted among the wealthy. Yet, we can't help but occasionally crave the excitement, the drama, and the attention given to someone who is truly exceptional.

Even in our faith, we tend to think of the saints and mystics as the superstars of the Church. We are not like them and never could be! They are the extraordinary ones, the special ones, who performed amazing feats of asceticism and virtue, or who received remarkable gifts in prayer. These are people such as Teresa of Avila, whose life seems filled with visions and ecstasies, or the contemporary Teresa of Calcutta, who had no visions, but whose life still seems so exceptional.

But we—we are ordinary people living everyday lives filled with a multitude of tiny, mundane details. Just as in a garden, most of the days follow the same dull routine.

We have been deeply formed by the supremely visual experience of TV, movies, and Internet. These media tend to sensationalize events. And so when we hear of extraordinary experiences, in prayer or in daily life, we tend to assume that such experiences are deeper, more real, more true, and more in touch with God than our own. Or if occasionally we have such experiences ourselves, it is so easy, so tempting, to focus on them and ignore all the little, everyday ways in which God comes to us.

Yet, Ordinary Time takes up much of the liturgical year. There are only four weeks of Advent, one week of Christmas season, six weeks of Lent, and seven weeks of Easter, yet there are thirty-four weeks of Ordinary Time. That seems to accurately reflect our lives, doesn't it? We also have occasional major events and happenings, but most of it is all very prosaic. The very length of Ordinary Time signals its importance to us. The Church seems to appreciate it, even enjoy it. But do we? For that matter, why should we?

Perhaps the key words here are "extraordinary" and "ordinary." When we believe that God comes to us only in extraordinary times and experiences, we limit ourselves and God. While these moments may be valuable, and they certainly command our attention, they are usually unpredictable and so beyond our control. In fact, we have experience of God that is much more accessible and available: our common day-to-day experience. Filled with God's hidden presence and life, it is available always, at every moment. The texture of our simple daily experience is the privileged place of God's presence. We need only to become more aware of it.

Ordinary Time and ordinary space: this is where we find God. Yet, it also seems to be the place where nothing much ever seems to happen. It's entirely too familiar, even boring. What do we do on these days? In a garden, it's weeding, or watering, or mulching, or thinning, or picking, or any of a number of simple, repetitive tasks that get done again and again at various times throughout the year. Cooking, cleaning, doing dishes—these are all the tasks of Ordinary Time. Answering the phone, writing letters, paying bills, going to work and coming home, perhaps commuting in heavy traffic—all these are things that we do thousands of times. Shopping, shoveling snow, cleaning the bathroom—these may be our least favorite tasks, but they all need doing, not once and for all, but over and over and over.

These are the tasks and the times that we want to hurry through so as to get on to something more important, more satisfying, and more exciting. The liturgical year continues to insist, quietly and firmly, that Ordinary Time is important. It is not to be rushed through so as to get on to Christmas or Easter. Instead of looking to the future, and to momentous events, it focuses us on the here and now of everyday life.

"The present moment is always overflowing with immeasurable riches, far more than you are able to hold." So wrote Jean-Pierre de Caussade, in his classic work, *Abandonment to Divine Providence.*[1] "You [God] speak to every individual through what happens to them moment by moment," he continues. "Instead of hearing the voice of God in all these things and revering the mysterious obscurity of his word, however, men [sic] see in them only material happenings, the effects of chance or purely human activities."[2]

Why is it that we can't recognize that our humdrum daily lives and experiences offer us the entry into God's presence? Our minds are filled with thoughts of all the many things we need to do and accomplish. Our hearts are burdened with the weight of years past: things left undone, things regretted. Or our thoughts launch us into the future with fear of what is to come or dreams of what might someday be. Rarely do we focus on the simple place where we are right now. Yet, it is only here and now in the present—*this* time, *this* place, *these* thoughts, *this* task—where God waits for *us* to be present.

"We can find all that is necessary in the present moment," Caussade tells us.[3] But how hard it is for us to accept this, how persistently we resist. We think of this as a formula for resignation to injustices, large and small. At the very least, we think, it is an invitation to passivity. Another writer, a contemporary who brings Buddhist insight to the situation, negates this possibility. "Remind yourself that acceptance of the present moment has nothing to do with resignation in the face of what is happening. It simply means a clear acknowledgment that *what is happening is happening.* Acceptance doesn't tell you what to do."[4]

These writers, as well as the yearly weeks of Ordinary Time, remind us that it is vital to be present to our moments, our thoughts, and our actions, no matter how trivial or unimportant. It is our presence that is so important—or, as the Buddhist tradition names it, our mindfulness. "Mindfulness means paying attention in a particular way: on purpose, in the present moment, and nonjudgmentally. This kind of attention nurtures greater awareness, clarity, and acceptance of present-moment reality. It wakes us up to the fact that our lives unfold only in moments. If we are not fully present for many of those moments, we may not only miss what is most valuable in our lives but also fail to realize the richness and the depth of our possibilities for growth and transformation."[5]

The opposite of mindfulness is that nearly habitual state of half-attention, which is referred to as "autopilot." So many of our moments are spent unaware, only half-conscious. We even make a goal out of this and speak with pride of our ability to multitask. But if we are not deeply and fully present to anyone or anything, our attention is divided, scattered, and dispersed. Most of all, we are not present to ourselves.

_eeee

Robert Frost once neatly put it this way:

> I turned to speak to God
> About the world's despair
> But to make bad matters worse
> I found God wasn't there.
>
> God turned to speak to me
> (don't anybody laugh)
> God found I wasn't there
> At least not over half.[6]

This may strike us as funny, and it is, but it is also sad. For God is only present to us here and now, in the present moment. God does not relate to the person we'd like to be, or the person we hope someday we will become. God doesn't directly relate to us through future or past events. God relates to us as we are now, right here in the present moment and the present circumstances, however wonderful or awful or even dull. If we are not present to ourselves, we cannot be present to God.

How do we know God is present? The Christian scriptures clearly tell us through John's great final discourse, "I will ask the Father, and he will give you another Advocate, to be with you forever. This is the Spirit of truth. . . . *He abides with you, and he will be in you*" (Jn 14:16, 17; emphasis added).

The presence of this Spirit with us is real presence. It is with us constantly, though usually unseen, unfelt, unacknowledged. It is also hard to isolate, sliding through our grasping minds and hearts, out of the clutch of our yearning neediness, yet hovering, like a butterfly or hummingbird, showering us with nectar in surprising ways when we are open and aware. Scripture scholar Samuel Terrien once described the Spirit as an "elusive presence."

So elusive is it that often we call it absence! Ordinary Time, when we live this time mindfully, can make us deeply aware of God's apparent absence. Could this possibly be a form of presence? Doris Grumbach, a recent author who named her book *The Presence of Absence,* must surely think so. One of the hallmarks of daily experience is that it is always changing, always fluctuating. It alternates between times of great presence and times of great absence. Absence in particular has the potential to lead us more directly to awareness of our reality as finite, limited, burdened beings. Through this we open ourselves more deeply to our need for the divine presence. One of the giants of Christian mysticism, St. Bernard, tells us, "When the soul feels an inflowing of grace, it recognizes his presence; when it does not, it complains of his absence and seeks his return, saying with the Psalmist: 'My face has sought you; your face, Lord, will I seek.'"[7]

The Eucharist is a potent symbol for the presence of God in ordinary times and places, for under the appearance of the everyday reality of bread and wine, God is powerfully present. Catholics take this so easily for granted and forget that it is not only a sacrament, but a reminder and image for God's hidden yet living presence in all the everyday realities of life.

This hidden presence, so abundantly available to us moment by moment in both presence and absence, is what Ordinary Time persistently tries to reveal. It is the heart and soul of our encounter with God. Perhaps, if we open ourselves to our daily experience, if we are mindful, we may find that elusive presence waiting there for us. Mindful presence may open up into Presence. We may come to recognize that presence is not only ordinary; it is deeply filled with God. To speak of this presence is even to speak of mysticism, of intimate contact with God.

"I looked, and there in heaven a door stood open!" (Rv 4:1). So writes the seer of the book of Revelation. This door to the kingdom of heaven is wide open—and it is right here on earth. As Jesus said, the kingdom is God's presence among us. Once Jesus was asked by the Pharisees when the kingdom of God was coming, and he answered, "The kingdom of God is not coming with things that can be observed; nor will they say, 'Look, here it is!' or 'There it is!' For, in fact, the kingdom of God is among you" (Lk 17:20–21). The kingdom of God is among you! It is not in some far-off future time and place or in some extraordinary event, but it is among you—or, as some translations say, "within you." Jesus uses images for the kingdom as well. They are almost always small and simple: a pearl hidden in a field, a lost coin, leaven in bread, a mustard seed—and again and again, the kingdom is a meal celebrated among family and friends.

Our lives are filled with ordinary time, ordinary people, and ordinary events. We lose treasures in fields and homes; and find them again. We knead leaven into bread; we knead the leaven of vitality; and imagination into the most humdrum of tasks; we knead the leaven of love into difficult and challenging relationships. We plant seeds in the garden and water and weed; and we plant seeds of hope and trust into our lives and others' as well, watering and weeding with faith and love and patience. In all these ordinary ways, the kingdom of God's loving presence is elusively entwined into the most ordinary of time.

ah,
roses!

Back about fourteen or fifteen years ago, I opened
the pages of the latest edition of *Horticulture* magazine, and fell head over heels in love. It was sometime in midwinter, when everyone in Maine is
longing for warm sun, green grass, and most of all
flowers. And there, as the centerfold, was a gorgeous spread of David Austin's English roses. It
was my first acquaintance, and it was love at first
sight.

English roses, the article proudly proclaimed,
were a new breed, the fruit of the lifetime work
of English hybridizer David Austin breeding
old-fashioned roses—with their wonderful fragrance, hundreds of petals, charm of form and
shape, and weather hardiness—with hybrid teas:
those aristocrats of the cut-flower trade, bred for

repeat bloom and marvelous color, but alas, with little or no fragrance. Hybrid teas, unfortunately, tend to stick up on their long, sturdy stems from little shrubs that are, well, not the most beautiful, to put it tactfully. Plus, they are not hardy enough to withstand the rigors of a Maine winter. Old-fashioned roses have wonderful fragrance, and they are often displayed on lovely shrubs: arching, climbing, graceful shrubs. But most of them only bloom once a season.

These new English roses were reputedly much more hardy than hybrid teas, wonderfully fragrant, with the lovely gracious layers of petals of the old-fashioned roses—and they kept blooming all summer. The photos were wonderful! How could I help but fall in love? Once fallen, I could only surrender to the inevitable: purchase them, and plant them, and love them.

Now, fourteen years later, with the old garden long gone and in a new home at last with new gardens to tend and new fields to till—the same roses bloom in the new garden and the same ones, and more. There are new rosebushes, but some of the same names, and surely the same beauty of form and fragrance. There is one of pinky-peach, one of deep, dark, passionate red, one of meltingly glorious gold—and another a porcelain, clear, palest of pink, its outer petals alabaster, enclosing the inner, deeper pink in a perfectly shaped chalice, a cup of perfect purity. And fragrance! The entire cloister is scented with roses: delicate, not overpowering, just sufficient to lend an aura of something different, something special, to this lovely enclosed space.

Ah, roses! Perhaps they are the ultimate image of love. We send them on Valentine's Day, on Mother's Day, on birthdays and anniversaries. We twine them into wedding bouquets, and we send them with the coffin on its way to the grave—the last, lonely image of our undying love.

Ah, roses. Glorious roses, lovely roses: in flower form they are the ultimate image of love. But whose love? Human love? Perhaps so, for they are no doubt beautiful, fragrant, and truly lovely. Glorious roses have hundreds and hundreds of petals, dense and rich and velvety, so tightly entwined with one another that it's impossible to find the center of the bloom. Could this be why they are the symbol of human love? For they so beautifully represent the human heart! And who can truly know the human heart? It holds layer upon layer of depth: depth of memory, depth of motivation, depth of emotion, and yes, even depth of weakness and frailty. Even our own heart is a mystery to us! "I the Lord test the mind and search the heart, to give to all according to their ways" (Jer 17:10). Only the Lord truly knows our heart. Yet, we know that our desires are what drive us, and love is the deepest desire of our heart. What is it that we desire? Or *who* is it? Layer upon layer, depth upon depth. Our loves, our desires, our passion, must be transformed if we would love purely, beautifully, sincerely. Even as a rose, or indeed any plant or flower, is simply what it is without false pretense or circumvention, so must we be. But for us it is hard work. We cover our heart with layer upon layer of defense, posturing, illusions, obsessions, and sinfulness. Layer upon layer, depth upon depth, day by day, year after year, we work at the transformation. The layers of a rose's petals are simply and purely rose. Often, our layers are those of fallenness, falseness, and sin. To find the heart of a rose, even one as dense and deep as an English rose, is relatively easy. To find our heart, to find the jewel that we have clouded over, takes a lifetime.

As any gardener knows, to plant a rose is only the beginning. To tend a rose and make it flourish takes work. We plant and fertilize, we manure and mulch, we weed and water and tend. And so it is with ourselves. We need to tend ourselves, tend the rose plant that is our life, if we would blossom in the right season. As with roses, we do this not by ourselves alone, not merely by our own effort. We do this hand in hand with God, who alone gives the growth. For it is God who works with our cooperation to transform the human heart.

But perhaps there is more to it than this. True, the rose is a wonderful symbol of human love. Yet, it is also a symbol of God's love. Perhaps this is why these roses speak so deeply to my heart. "In this is love, not that we loved God, but that he loved us," says St. John. "We love because he first loved us" (1 Jn 4:10, 19).

I think of the work that love involves, and the fidelity, and the perseverance. Real love is not a passing infatuation. St. Paul tells us that love abides forever. Like the work of tending roses, it is not for the fainthearted, nor for those who want something quick and easy. To gain those gorgeous blooms—in the garden or in our lives—takes constant work and tending.

I look back on my life now, after several decades of working and struggling to follow God's teachings, God's writings, God's movements in my heart and in my life, and I am overwhelmed by the constant, loving fidelity that God has shown me. The prophet Ezekiel gives us the image—the gruesome image—of who we have been as individuals and as a people. The image is that of an abandoned infant, covered in blood, unloved, thrown out in the field to die. And as Ezekiel reports the Lord's words, he continues:

> I passed by you, and saw you flailing about in your blood. As you lay in your blood, I said to you, "Live!" and grow up like a plant of the field. . . . I passed by you again and looked on you; you were at the age for love. I spread the edge of my cloak over you, and covered your nakedness. I pledged myself to you and entered into a covenant with you, says the Lord God, and you became mine. Then I bathed you with water and washed all the blood from you, and anointed you with oil. I clothed you with embroidered cloth and with sandals of fine leather; I bound you in fine linen and covered you with rich fabric. (Ez 16:6, 8–10)

This image, graphic in both its brutality and its loveliness, was given to Ezekiel as an image of the unfaithful people of Israel and the immense tender fidelity of God. It is an image of each one of us, abandoned infants covered in the blood of our woundedness, whether received from others or self-inflicted. Yet, God's tender love and compassion reaches out to us and heals us, covers us over, dresses us in the beautiful robes of virtues and gifts, and slowly brings us back to health and life and beauty.

I remember. I remember well my difficult beginnings as a literary child, a child who loved nature and solitude and depth, born into a family who did their best to love and care for me, but who were lamentably, unfailingly different. Born into a family where my older siblings seemed to care mostly for cars and speed and glitter. Born into an inarticulate family, and so it took decades as an adult to learn how to articulate as I needed. Born into a wounded, dysfunctional family—as most of us are!—where I learned to bury my emotions so deeply that I didn't even know what they were. Born into a family where I was constantly told I was the bright one, the star, and so I learned, alas, that I had to be a star—even though my real tendency is to quiet and solitude.

I remember. And I also remember that God put me into a family on a farm, in the country, in nature. I remember long solitary walks surrounded by trees and meadows. I remember playing by the brook behind the fields and loving its constant chatter, sometimes a soft chuckle, sometimes a throaty roar. I loved its look in winter, threaded with ice, or in spring with clumps of bloodroots and marsh marigolds tucked into its folds. I loved it in full summer when it hardly whispered as it slowly glided serenely along its way, hiding itself demurely under cover of the overhanging trees and large dark ferns. I loved the blazing scarlet cardinal flower that surprised me by its banks one summer. I loved and was loved by God's gracious hand in his tender, gorgeous creation.

I remember the garden. I loved the garden, though as a child I didn't care much for pulling weeds or planting seedlings. I loved the smell of the tomatoes as they ripened in the sun. I loved cutting open a cantaloupe, ripe and warm in the hot sun, and eating it with a jackknife. I loved the raspberries and the high-bush blueberries. God clothed me with the garment of the garden, and I snuggled into its warm comfort.

I remember. Clearly I remember the geese that we kept, and the ganders who terrified me. But I also remember, dimly, being taught to write very young, with a goose quill pen. I remember being read to, and I've been told—though I don't remember—that at age three I either knew my stories by heart or else could really read them to my parents. I remember being absent from class one day in third grade when a forest ranger came to speak. The next day, when I was back in class, we all had to write thank-you letters. I remember that I miraculously (or so it seems now) had the wit to say, "Though I wasn't here, I heard how good your talk was, and I'm sorry I missed it." My letter wasn't chosen to send to him, but it was good enough to be one of several read aloud by the teacher. I remember how proud I was of that.

I remember the set of sixteen big, red books my parents bought for us when I was still very young. The first volume had *The Wagner Children* printed on it in gold letters! Book one was the easiest, at a learning-to-read level. The others went in ascending order right up through book sixteen, which was for teenagers. I remember reading through all of them—devouring them, actually—long before I was a teen. And I'm grateful for the parents who weren't particularly articulate themselves but who wanted me to read, who wanted me to be educated.

I remember. I remember the big, empty gallon coffee can, all washed and cleaned and gleaming, with a slit punctured in its lid. This was my piggy bank, and it was for my college education. I remember a family that couldn't contain me, that didn't know what to do with me, but only wanted the best for me and tried to plan for that best to happen.

I remember those miserable, unhappy high school years, when I wasn't pretty, wasn't popular, wasn't thin—oh, how well I remember! I remember signing up for Mr. Lawn's European History class, which even gave me some college credits. I remember the nine of us in that class, and what a terrific class it was. I learned how to think! I read a history of ideas! And I was introduced to Catholicism, and my world suddenly changed.

Writing about it now today, I can only say thank you to the Lord for coming into my life and transforming it. I learned to think and I learned about faith at one and the same time. Oh, what a blessed gift of God's providential loving care! How well you knew what I needed, and how well you provided for it.

And now I remember, with an adult's memory, my challenging college years when I rode the roller coaster of belief and unbelief, and then my year in seminary when I finally surrendered and knew, with all my heart and soul and strength, that I *needed* the Lord. In the midst of this chaos, I remember with wonder those early-morning Old Testament classes with a professor who loved the scriptures and who imparted that love to me. I remember Sr. Laetitia, who accidentally or providentially lived in the dorm just across the hall from me and who became my mentor and friend. I remember the Catholic church just down the hill—still left open in those more innocent years— where I found the flame of my heart nurtured and fulfilled.

I remember Carmel, and the challenges and struggles of those years, with a crazy prioress and a tangle of half-crazy, half-healthy spiritual formation. And yet, there was unbelievably fierce joy as well, joy in the simplest, tiniest of things, which would come upon me for no reason at all: sunlight on the bare floor of the recreation room, or when I was walking down the path by the statue of St. Joseph one day, and for no reason gratitude and thankfulness leapt in my heart. I remember leaving Carmel, and the bitter anguish, for how could I leave what was dearer to me than life itself? And yet, the Lord was leading me out, out into the desert of I knew not where. How I remember! And it was God's love that led me.

And then began the long, lonely search for where I was to go and what I was to do, and all the while—through the people you brought into my life, and the books that I found, and the immense turmoil, and the learning of so many adult responsibilities, and the lostness of having my world collapse and needing to resurrect it from scratch—love was guiding me, through the darkness, through the fear, through the struggle—weeding and watering and tending—and slowly, ever so slowly, disentangling those rose petals that encased my heart with an iron grip, and letting them slowly, ever so slowly open to light and life and love.

> Be still, deadening north wind
> South wind come, you that waken love,
> Breathe through my garden,
> Let its fragrance flow,
> And the Beloved will feed amid the flowers.[1]

Even as roses need shelter from the bitter north winds of winter, even as they awaken to the warmth of a summer breeze, so, too, do we need to shelter ourselves from the bitterness of our fallen habits, obsessions, and compulsions. So do we need to bask in the breath of the Spirit, which warms us into light and life.

It takes time to grow roses. It takes time, and patience, and lots of hard work. And it takes time to grow a life toward God—time and patience and hard work. Most of all, it takes love: God's love and human love, entangled and entwined, working together in the Spirit.

Yes, it takes time, work, and openness to what God alone can give. And God alone gives us roses: fragrant, velvety, rich, lush; emblem of love, human and divine; emblem of the human heart.

A garden locked is my sister, my bride,
a garden locked, a fountain sealed.
Your channel is an orchard of pomegranates
    with all choicest fruits,
    henna with nard,
nard and saffron, calamus and cinnamon,
    with all trees of frankincense,
myrrh and aloes,
    with all chief spices—
a garden fountain, a well of living water,
and flowing streams from Lebanon.

Awake, O north wind,
    and come, O south wind!
Blow upon my garden
    that its fragrance may be wafted abroad.
Let my beloved come to his garden,
    and eat its choicest fruits. (Sg 4:12–16)

japanese beetles

I spotted the first one on the Fourth of July, and my heart plummeted. There it was, that greenish-brown iridescent bug. Although the first, it was certainly not the last, of that I was sure. They first arrived last summer, in mid-July—first on the roses in the cloister garden, then on the plum trees and the cherry trees, then on the basil. Oh, no! There they were, on all my favorite plants! Hundreds upon hundreds, thousands upon thousands of them.

I had hardly ever seen them before, having previously lived farther north. But every year, the *Fedco* catalog assured me, they march farther north. And now, with our little hermitage newly transferred farther *south*, we were right in Japanese beetle territory.

And so, here they are: Japanese beetles. I suppose that somewhere they must play an important part in the ecology of the place. They must have their approved and necessary niche. Perhaps something in their life cycle keeps some other bug, or some plant, or some fungus in control. And something else, no doubt, keeps them under control. But here in Windsor, Maine, as elsewhere in America, they are totally out of control.

I complain, loudly, to anyone who will listen. I pray, fervently. I set up traps. Almost, *almost*, I am tempted to use pesticides. But then I see ladybugs, those wonderful and beneficial garden insects, on the same rugosa roses that the Japanese beetles love so much, and I hold off. What kills the beetles will also kill the ladybugs. I go on "beetle brigade" four times a day, picking them off the roses, the newly planted flowering crabs, the bayberry, the basil. I can't even begin to get them off the upper reaches of the plum and cherry trees. Then I notice the wild cherries, which are everywhere around us—and they also have Japanese beetles! And I think, this is hopeless. It is just overwhelming.

Milky spore, injected foot by foot into the lawns, will gradually exterminate them by killing the grubs in which they overwinter. I quail at the thought. We have a fair amount of lawn and a much larger hayfield. How can I possibly inject it, foot by foot, with milky spore? Plus, the directions specify that it's best to do this on a neighborhood-wide basis for true efficacy. While our neighbors are acres away instead of just a few yards, they still are neighbors. And they also have lawns and fields that will harbor those damned grubs. It is just overwhelming.

Beetle brigade begins the first week of July and continues through August. Early morning, mid-morning, early afternoon, evening, I inspect the roses, bush by bush, tin can in my hand, filled with soapy water. I shake the beetles into it, where they die. Some escape, but I get plenty. Early the next morning, I toss out the water and dead beetles, fill it again, and begin again.

St. Benedict's feast day, July 11, comes and goes—a lovely day filled with prayer and song. It is a joyous day, celebrating our *Rule*, its writer St. Benedict, and our rich spiritual heritage. It's a day to celebrate and rejoice and give thanks to God—and to persevere in picking off Japanese beetles. *Suscipe.* "Uphold me and I shall live, according to your promise." So we chant and pray when we make our vows. *Suscipe.* From the Latin verb *suscipio,* it means: "take," "receive," "accept," "uphold," "undertake," "protect," "guard," "support," "lift up." And so, remembering, I pray on St. Benedict's day: uphold me, protect me, receive me. Uphold me today, and tomorrow, and the day after that. Uphold me in this unending, uphill battle against these voracious insects. Uphold me in this daily, unending, uphill battle against myself.

A friend of mine, a monk now long departed from this life, once remarked that as a teenager he had become a believer, and "ever since then, I have been daily at war." I was younger then and let his words slip over my head. But something inside must have been awakened, for they remained deep in my memory. I think of them often now, and especially when making my daily harvest of Japanese beetles. I am often angry with these bugs: angry and frustrated and powerless. Perhaps it is easier to feel angry than to feel powerless, and so I grow angry. Nothing I can do will stop them. It seems as though all the thousands I kill make no incursions against their depredations. They go straight for the rosebuds and latch on to them, chewing away at the petals, hollowing out the center of the bud. Sometimes there are as many as a dozen on one rose, or even more on a cluster of the rugosas.

Yet, anger does no good. It is a poison, insidious—as if the hated beetles are chewing away inside me. Daily I am at war, like Anthony in his desert cave, engaged in the "singlehanded combat of the desert." Anthony contended with the demons, and with the grace of God he won. I contend mostly with myself. Uphold me, Lord, and I shall live. Like Anthony, if you uphold me, I, too, shall live. Uphold me. *Suscipe.*

Unlike Anthony, I am not aware of contending with demons. I can't even vanquish these bugs, nor can I vanquish my own anger. According to the fifth-century monastic author John Cassian, this "deadly poison of anger . . . must be totally uprooted from the depths of our soul. For as long as it resides in our hearts . . . we shall not be sharers in life . . . and certainly not receptive to the spiritual and true light."[1]

It is indeed a deadly poison. Once infected, my mind takes irascible flight, the slightest of pretexts gives rise to my furious contempt and ire, and all calm, all sanity, all rationality are gone. The excuses for anger are legion, like the pig-inhabiting demons of Gospel fame. Someone didn't answer me properly, or someone is complaining again, or else the weather is awful, or there's an animal who dares to eat my just-ripening melons! And, of course, the weeds are worse than ever this year. And who is it who keeps leaving the door open, and letting all the flies in? How dare they! Or why does the phone ring just when we're beginning lunch? Or—my biggest target—those *damned* hoses. Truly an invention of the devil, always tangling and bending back on themselves, they *always* need to be straightened out before the water can flow.

Day in, day out, year after year, the same things get to me. Day after day, year after year, the poison of anger flows. It insinuates itself into relationships, into plans, into trust and hope and love. Cassian is right when he says that it blinds us and places a wall between ourselves and the Spirit. Current psychology tells us that anger has its positive uses—for instance, we should be angry at injustice. Yet, Cassian will not allow even this—could he possibly be right? He comments on those who say that, in the Bible, God is often portrayed as angry or even vengeful. His answer to this? That God is often portrayed in human form: with arms, or with a head of white hair, or with eyes, or sometimes as sleeping or even drunk. Do we really believe this is anything other than a metaphor? Of course not! So then, is not the anger, too, a metaphor?

For what, then, are we allowed to be angry, since anger must be given us for some purpose? We should be angry over our own failings, he says, if indeed we must be angry. But it is best of all "to root out the movements of wrath." For in anger, "the guiding principle of our heart is obscured by darkness; and then . . . it can never become a temple of the Holy Spirit as long as the spirit of wrath dwells in us."[2]

This sounds like a tall order, way too much for me. Yet, the world is so filled with anger; surely that is not good. Contrary to this, many people must learn not to suppress the anger they have held down for so long. Surely that, too, is necessary, for repressed anger is the worst of poisons. One common understanding of depression is anger turned inward. Other voices from the monastic tradition find positive uses for anger; though like Cassian, they believe it must be not an intemperate, impulsive wrath, but delivered out of forethought and calm.

I know well from experience that an angry mind and heart drive out the Spirit. How impossible it is to be truly open and receptive to God when I am filled with anger! Wrath is not only consuming; it is filling. Receptivity to the Spirit implies openness, readiness—really, a kind of blessed emptiness. "A heart that has been emptied . . . gives birth to divine, mysterious intellections that sport within it like fish and dolphins in a calm sea. The sea is fanned by a soft wind, the heart by the Holy Spirit," says Hesychios.[3] Most of all, our hearts need peacefulness—the very opposite of anger.

And so I return to the cloister and its sheltered garden. Despite the beetles, it embraces me with its peace. I take up the beetle brigade: early morning, mid-morning, early afternoon, evening—rose by rose, bush by bush. July passes, August arrives. The moon waxes and wanes. The beetles wax and wane also. Perhaps a hidden blessing in all this is that I daily get to inspect the plants and see how they are doing. Daily I am brought into close contact with these lovely little pieces of God's enchanting creation. And daily, many times daily, I have the opportunity—if only, *if only*, I can remember to take it—to practice patience and forbearance, and to remember that I, too, am only one small element in God's creation. Japanese beetles do not need to be overwhelming. Nor do other people need to be overwhelming. Nor does anything, not even my own anger. *Suscipe.* Uphold me, Lord, and I shall live, according to your Word.

walking on water

From May 1 through July 17 we received only about four inches of rain—much, much less than normal. On July 18 we had a good shower, which signaled the end of our incipient drought. From July 18 through August 16, we received about a foot of rain. That's right, a foot: twelve inches. This occurred at a time that is normally Maine's driest. There was even a week when it rained six out of seven days. Many of the rains were small: one- or two-tenths of an inch at most. But others were torrential downpours. One left us with an inch and a half of rain, all within about an hour.

At the southwest corner of the cloister garden, just behind the cloister itself, and to the right of where we hope to build our permanent chapel, is the bell tower. A simple structure, it consists of three slender poles, rising toward each other, and joining in a small, sloping roof. The bell that calls us to prayer several times each day hangs from this roof, and a rope falls down toward a small raised floor, with a bench at the bottom. During one of these recent deluges, I happened to be bell ringer, and it was time to ring for Vespers. I came out of my cell to find that the lawn that surrounds the central garden and the bell tower was under about an inch of water. More was pouring down, and the water was getting deeper. I didn't want to pull on boots, and I didn't want to get soaked, so I took the coward's way out and ran around knocking on doors, safe under the shelter of the cloister roof.

The next morning, the Gospel for the day was Matthew 14:22–33. It's about the disciples out in the boat at night during a storm. In the midst of it, Jesus comes to them, walking on the water. They are afraid, yet he reassures them: "It is I; do not be afraid" (Mt 14:27). Peter, the impulsive one, promptly asks the Lord to bid him come to him over the water, and Jesus does so. Peter gets out of the boat, begins walking, looks down, gets scared, and begins to sink. Jesus, of course, pulls him out.

The obvious meaning of the story is about faith: our need for it, our lack of it. But somehow, this time—with the image fresh in my mind of the cloister under an inch of water, and my reluctance to walk out into it—the old meaning took on fresh life for me.

Perhaps I've always thought of walking on water as an extraordinary event. Given the Gospel story, it would seem to be. But my life is short on extraordinary events, and long on the ordinary. This seems to be true for most of us, and so it can be hard to relate to this story personally. Yet I'd just been confronted with the opportunity to walk on water, and turned it down. Only an inch of water perhaps, yet nonetheless. . . .

Perhaps walking on water is more common than I'd once thought. In fact, when we consider our lives of faith nowadays, perhaps it's what we're called to do every single time we operate out of the motivation of faith instead of all the ordinary human motives, such as utility, pleasure, self-service, power, lust, anger—this list could go on forever.

Today we are drowning in materialism, hedonism, and pragmatism. The message that is continuously drilled into our heads in multitudinous ways is that *this* world is all there is. Granted, this may not be obvious. Our emphasis in education, in jobs, in government, even in psychology, is all about that which can be quantified, measured, and understood. It's also about the bottom line: how much it will cost. I have often thought that communism—that is, economic determinism—has in an insidious way won the battle with the so-called free world. Why? Because everything is always all about money and price and economics. Communism has succeeded in its negative emphasis, but completely failed in introducing its good goal: classless society, a utopia in which all are equally cared for and have equal opportunity.

But to return to the water, and our faith: here we are, drowning in a society of materialism, inundated with the subliminal message that this world is all there is. To counter this, to act out of our faith and not out of the promptings of this Madison Avenue–driven world, is a courageous, perhaps even foolhardy act—sort of like walking on water.

Remember that John Lennon lyric, "Imagine there's no heaven." Let's imagine the reverse: Imagine that there really is a God. Imagine that there is another world, more real than this one, and always very close to us. Imagine that other values—love, integrity, trust, hope, faith, courage, compassion—are possible and can make a difference. Imagine that prayer is not just words sent off into a void, but the sign of a real relationship, a loving relationship. Imagine that it's possible for people to live, not just occasionally, but permanently out of these values, and out of this faith. Just imagine: these people are walking on water every day of their lives.

Why do I say that? Because that's what faith is—walking on water, with our eyes fixed on Jesus, who calls to us from out of the storm of this life. Impulsive, like Peter, we want to do this unbelievable thing, want to take this unimaginable risk. But the waves are so large. The roar of this world, this life, this here and now, is enormous. In spite of everything, in all sorts of little ways, with our eyes and hearts intent on our faith, we manage somehow to walk on water. Most of us would not consider this anything remarkable, and yet it is.

Still, I think there's more to this story than our everyday walking on water. This story is recounted by Mark and John as well as Matthew. But Mark and John leave out the part about Peter walking on the waves. For these other evangelists, what is most important is that *Jesus* is walking on the water. There are other elements to consider as well. For instance, this happens at night on the water, far from land, in the midst of a great wind and storm. Mark tells us, "When evening came, the boat was out on the sea, and he was alone on the land. When he saw that they were straining at the oars against an adverse wind, he came towards them early in the morning, walking on the sea" (Mk 6:47–48). John tells us, "It was now dark, and Jesus had not yet come to them. The sea became rough because a strong wind was blowing" (Jn 6:17–18).

This picture evokes, indeed is no doubt meant to evoke, two other very vivid images from the Old Testament. The first image is from the very beginning of the Bible, from the opening chapter of Genesis. "In the beginning when God created the heavens and the earth, the earth was a formless void and darkness covered the face of the deep, while a wind from God swept over the face of the waters" (Gn 1:1–2). That mighty wind from God, sweeping over the waters, is another name for God's spirit: *ruach* in Hebrew, which means both "wind" and "spirit." In the midst of the darkness, over the formless waters of chaos, the wind of God breathed, and creation began to be. And now, in Matthew, Mark, and John there is another darkness, and another wind upon the stormy waters; and out of the chaos, Jesus appears, bringing order, peace, and as we shall see, a new creation. Three evangelists, writing from a variety of traditions, each in his own way, evokes the primeval darkness and waters from the beginning of God's creation. Each one exquisitely nudges us to notice that creation, in the person of Jesus, is being born anew.

In case we miss the point, we hear the resonances of the far more noticeable story of the new creation, the Resurrection story. Beginning the story of the Resurrection, Mark tells us it was, *"very early on the first day of the week"* (Mk 16:2; emphasis added). Similarly, it was early in the morning that Jesus walked on the water, signaling a new creation. And very early on the first day of the week (the same day in which God began to create), the women discover the empty tomb and the glorious, astonishing fact of resurrection.

The next image evoked is again from the Old Testament, this time from the book of Exodus. This is the famous night of the Passover, the night when the Lord, with mighty arm and outstretched hand, liberated the Israelites from slavery in Egypt, and brought them out, through the midst of the waters of the Red Sea, into freedom. "Then Moses stretched out his hand over the sea. The Lord drove the sea back by a strong east wind all night, and turned the sea into dry land; and the waters were divided. The Israelites went into the sea on dry ground, the waters forming a wall for them on their right and on their left" (Ex 14:21–22).

Fr. Bruno Barnhart, in his book *The Good Wine,* says this "exodus event was the birth of Israel as a people, the primordial act of God on their behalf which became the foundation stone of Israelite faith for all time. . . . The Passover sea-crossing is one of the principal Old Testament types, or symbolic foreshadowings, of the death and resurrection of Christ. Here at the crossing of the sea we begin to see the crucial phases of the history of Israel being taken up into the movement of the gospel and into the person of Jesus."[1] In this seemingly insignificant account of the walking on water—surely nothing all that remarkable when considered against the backdrop of Jesus' greater miracles—we find the great sweep of Old Testament history, from creation through the Exodus, evoked and encompassed in the person of Jesus. Here, in this passage of the crossing of the sea, we find reminiscences of so many Old Testament passages referring back to the Exodus:

> When the waters saw you, O God,
> when the waters saw you, they were afraid;
> the very deep trembled.
>
> . . . the earth trembled and shook.
> Your way was through the sea,
> your path, through the mighty waters;
> yet your footprints were unseen. (Ps 77.16, 18c–19)

Additionally we find that Jesus says a very remarkable thing in all of these accounts. He says, "It is I." In Matthew he says, "Take heart, it is I; do not be afraid" (Mt 14:27). In Mark it is the same. And in John he says, "It is I; do not be afraid" (Jn 6:20). This "it is I," the scripture scholars say, is one of the most remarkable statements in the entire Bible, whose first appearance comes long before the Gospels. The "it is I" translation of the NRSV is another way of saying "I am"; and "I am" was the extraordinary answer given to Moses when he asked God to tell him his name. God appeared to Moses out of the burning bush and commissioned him to deliver the Israelites out of their slavery in Egypt. Moses tried to find a way out of doing this difficult and dangerous task and as a last resort cannily asked God, "If I come to the Israelites and say to them, 'The God of your ancestors has sent me to you,' and they ask me, 'What is his name?' what shall I say to them?" (Ex 3:13). In the ancient world of Moses, to know the name of someone is to have power over that person. Moses gambles that God will not want to reveal his name, giving away his power, and therefore Moses will have an excuse not to go. But God is too adroit to fall into this trap. He gives Moses a name—but that name is mystery.

"God said to Moses, "I AM WHO I AM." He said further, "Thus you shall say to the Israelites, 'I AM has sent me to you.'" God also said to Moses, "Thus you shall say to the Israelites, 'The Lord, the God of your ancestors, the God of Abraham, the God of Isaac, and the God of Jacob, has sent me to you': This is my name forever, and this is my title for all generations" (Ex 3:14–15).

This "I AM" is the sacred name of God, the name so holy and so sacred that subsequent generations of Israelites would not even allow themselves to pronounce it. Yet, here on the lips of Jesus is this holiest of names—and Jesus applies it to himself.

Here, in this little, almost unnoticed story—a bridge between the feeding of the multitudes, and his discourses with the Pharisees (in Matthew and Mark), and his discourse on the bread of life (in

John)—we see Jesus, the Lord of creation, recapitulating the first Passover, and foreshadowing his own, later Passover, and announcing his true name, his divinity, to his startled and fearful disciples. What a truly amazing little narrative, so filled to the brim with meaning, depth, and wonder! As Fr. Barnhart notes, "It is the one who rose from the water as the Spirit descended upon him, who now walks on the sea like the creative Spirit that was upon the primeval waters. It is the one who "was before me," who says, "*I AM.*"[2]

Is it possible to find even more riches in this little account of walking on the water? Perhaps it is. Fr. Barnhart follows scripture scholar Peter Ellis in placing this little account at the very center and apex of John's Gospel. Sound strange? Perhaps, but perhaps not. Ellis has noticed that John makes use of the ancient literary strategy of chiasm. This is a device often used in the ancient world, in which the center of a narrative is enclosed—like the folded wings of a butterfly, or the stamen and pistils at the heart of a rose—in parallel lines of discourse, which radiate out from this center. Each line or paragraph has a matching line or paragraph on the obverse side of the center, and together they enfold and embrace the center, pointing to it, and thus highlighting and emphasizing its importance, meaning, and—in this case—mystery. Ellis finds that this seemingly insignificant account of the night sea-crossing of Jesus is the actual heart and center of John's gospel.

Whether or not this is so doesn't actually concern me. But I am intrigued by the thoughts of chiasm itself. I see that Jesus is the hub of the great chiasm that is all of life and creation. He is its center and its radiant heart. All of life, all of time, all of creation, radiates out from him like the petals of the rose. On the one side stands the Old Testament, indeed all of time prior to his coming in the flesh. Creation, Abraham, Passover, Exodus, the journey, the Promised Land, the kingdom, the prophets, exile, return—all can be seen by us today as pointing to the one center, still to come in the person of Jesus. And all of history from the time of his Incarnation, death, resurrection, and ascension, the sending of the Spirit, the forming of Church, the giving of the sacraments, right down to our time—indeed right down to *my* own life, *your* own life—all these are the other side of God's great chiasm. All point back to their center: the luminous person of Jesus.

Walking on water is what Jesus did at a moment of urgent necessity for his disciples; and it was also a moment of epiphany, a revelation of who he is and what all of God's salvation history is about. Walking on water is what we do also, each day of our lives, when we step out in faith. When we walk on water, all of our seemingly insignificant actions take on immense significance. Walking on water, we recapitulate in our lives the person and actions of Jesus. Walking on water, the garden tells me, is possible. Even in a storm. Even when drowning. Even when—especially when—we don't realize the amazing story we're caught up in.

good to be here

Pushing my way through the underbrush, I arrive at the rim of a long, steep ridge, just at the point where it falls away in a cliff. The sharp drop leaves a gap in the leafy canopy, an opening of brilliant sun and deep blue sky which has drawn me onward magnetically. Now, standing at the rim's edge, I look over the crowns of the trees below, and out toward the next heavily wooded ridge, where it rises abruptly to the southeast. It is a magical view. There is no one in sight, no track, no building; there's nothing but trees, sky, sun—and height and depth. Yet, it is all just a few hundred yards off our prayer trail, not a twenty-minute walk from the hermitage itself. I am alone with only myself and God, high on a mountain, facing into the brilliant sky, and it is the morning of the Transfiguration.

> Jesus took with him Peter and John and James,
> and went up on the mountain to pray. And
> while he was praying, the appearance of his face
> changed, and his clothes became dazzling white.
> (Lk 9:28–29)

I had taken some time off this morning to take a long, leisurely walk down the prayer trail. Pausing midway, where the trail nears our south boundary, I noticed, as I had many times before, the traces of another trail, nearly obscured by several years of growth. It led north, along the top of a plateau, bordering the hill as it plunged down to the east to flatten out into the wetlands along Bull Brook. Today, I finally decided to follow this old trail. After an easy, relatively flat walk, open in places, and overgrown in others, I finally came to the orange ribbon that flagged our north boundary. Turning east, to the downhill side, I noticed the gap in the trees and headed for it, to be rewarded with the sun on my face, a spectacular view, and solitude.

> Peter said to Jesus, "Master, it is good for us to
> be here; let us make three dwellings, one for you,
> one for Moses, and one for Elijah"—not knowing
> what he said. (Lk 9:33)

How hard it is to leave here, and how I wish to linger. The sun illumines my face, dazzling my eyes. How close the Transfiguration seems at this moment; how I wish the Lord would linger also, transforming me, enwrapping me in his radiance. Peter seems so like Mary in the garden, after the Resurrection, wanting to hold on to Jesus, to make him linger. "Let us build three dwellings." Not for Peter, James, and John—but for Jesus, Moses, and Elijah. "Please stay, Master," I can almost hear Peter say. "Don't go away. Let this moment continue forever."

I remain awhile, but duty calls, and work is waiting, up the hill. The day continues, a priest friend arrives to celebrate Mass, and a few other friends come for it also. We share tea and cookies with them after. Vespers is later today and has its own special antiphons and prayers. We linger here, the fragrance of incense filling the chapel as we sing, "May our prayers rise before you, O Lord, as incense in your sight. . . . May this incense rise before you, may your mercy come down upon us."

The psalms this evening are short and beautiful: "on the holy mountains. From the womb of the morning, like dew, your youth will come to you" (Ps 110:3b). The second psalm also: "I lift up my eyes to the hills—from where will my help come? My help comes from the Lord, who made heaven and earth" (Ps 121:1–2). Between them, we pause in silence to linger awhile with the psalms and with the Lord who uses these psalms to speak to our hearts.

Such pauses between the psalms were normal in the early Church, but then fell out of use as the centuries passed. When I first entered religious life, there was a very different mentality toward the Liturgy of the Hours (or Divine Office, shortened to Office). In common with nearly all religious communities, the Office was *said* (not *prayed*!) from beginning to end without stopping. No pauses, no lingering. It was mandatory to say it completely,

without missing or changing a single word. A
friend who visited recently noticed that we pray
the psalms relatively slowly, with pauses between
each one. She asked about it, noting how much she
liked it, and said, "Back when I was in religious life,
the Office was something you began and galloped
your way through, hardly pausing for a breath until
the end. " Then she added, "Most communities still
do it this way."

It brought back memories! Indeed that's how
we said the Office when I first entered. But the Second Vatican Council brought reform, renewal, and
most of all a return to the sources. For Benedictines,
this means the *Rule* of Benedict and the traditions
of early Church. A veritable explosion of scholar-
ship—which had already been gathering steam—
took place, and gradually the monasteries absorbed
the new understandings and changed.

The change meant, in many ways, a return to
the traditions of early monastics. For amazingly
enough to us today, the Office, in those early centuries, didn't just consist of psalms, readings, and
spoken prayers. Yes, these were all major compo-
nents. But the Office also contained leisurely pauses
for silence and prayer: pauses to linger, between the
psalms and between the readings, and ponder, and
reflect, and talk to God in the heart. Adalbert de
Vogue, the famous scholar of the *Rule,* in an article
titled "The Divine Office," has this to say: "For the
ancients the office was by no means a mere decla-
mation of texts. Silent prayer occupied a consider-
able place in it." Further, "Prayer is the crowning
of the psalm."[1]

"What then is the proper role of psalmody at the office?" he asks. "It prepares for prayer, it invites one to pray."[2] We pause and linger and let a word or phrase unfold, expand, and settle in our hearts and minds. The psalm has opened us up, slowed us down, and granted us receptivity; the silence gives us time for the word to take root in the receptive earth of our listening souls. "The psalmody, preceding the prayer, not only resounds as the word of God inviting to prayer, it also guides the prayer which it has aroused."[3] Or, as Michael Casey writes, "The important thing during psalmody, therefore, is to remain vulnerable before the Psalm, ready to receive what its text and the operation of the Holy Spirit inspire."[4]

This evening of the Transfiguration, I wish to linger longer than time allows between the psalms. "Let us build three booths," I think. But the psalms and readings continue, followed by the Magnificat, and the intercessions. Vespers ends; this glorious day is winding down. The door from the chapel opens into the cloister, and this evening the Oriental lilies are in full and splendid bloom. Their rich fragrance drifts seductively on the warm, still air. I pause awhile and sit on the bench overlooking the garden. It is too delicious to resist, too difficult to keep myself moving on to collation and chores and whatever else is waiting this evening. I simply must linger among the color and scent and setting sun.

I think of Mary, commended by the Lord for sitting and listening at his feet. I think of Robert Frost, stopping by those snowy woods. I think, even more primally, of the Lord God, walking in the garden in the evening. It is good to linger. It is good to build booths, at least for a while. It is good—it is so very good to be here.

In the midst of busy and active lives, it is tough to linger. It's hard to find the time, and it's also very hard simply to slow down. We multitask; we live our lives full speed ahead. Slowing down, pausing, lingering: these are not usually understood to be virtues in our society. Worse, we move so fast, and have so much to do, that we have even forgotten how to linger. We are unable to slow down anymore.

For many years, even though time for prayer was built into my daily life, I had difficulty moving psychologically from slow time to fast time, from prayer time to work time. I would get too slowed down and couldn't get myself back into work mode. Or I would get going too fast and furious and couldn't seem to slow down when it was time for prayer.

Learning from the early monastic tradition, I now realize, has over the years helped me to make the transition more gracefully. The Office itself, when prayed with times and places for silence, slows me down. The psalms and scripture readings open me up and help me make the emotional transition from the functional world to the realm of the spirit. Lectio has progressively become, not just "spiritual reading"—a bit like reading a newspaper, but with a spiritual subject—but a slow, reflective, recitative pondering on the scriptural texts. I've also come to realize that nature itself helps me move away from the workaday world of tasks and duties into a slower mode, an opening to the window into God that creation is.

The reverse transition seems to come more easily, too, and that also is due to learning from the spiritual traditions of early monasticism, especially meditation. According to the early Church, meditation was not primarily discursive, a matter of the head, as has been the understanding of the last few centuries in the Christian world. Rather, somewhat akin to the Buddhist tradition, it was the slow, repetitive reiteration of a text, a line, or a word from the scriptures. Over and over the text gets repeated until slowly it lodges deep in the heart and remains there.

Recently at Vigils a line from a psalm blazed up out of the darkness of the predawn hours and into my heart: "Your consolation calms my soul." It returned, and I repeated it, again and again, throughout the hours of the day, which was filled with people, work, and distraction. "Your consolation calms my soul."

The transition to work becomes easier when scriptures such as this—line by line, or word by word—accompany me on my day. In the early Church, "recitation of the Word of God was a commonplace observance. It served to support a prayer which continued amidst occupations."[5]

Thus, the tension between work and prayer is not so hard-edged: moments of lingering pop up in the midst of a busy day, and eternity opens up and blossoms momentarily here and there, when least expected. "Your consolation calms my soul."

Perhaps our life here, with elements of both solitude and community, reflects this ever-present tension between work and activity on the one hand, and prayer, solitude, and receptivity on the other. It's hard to get the balance right, and we're constantly adjusting. Perhaps the balance is to be found in those very adjustments, and in the constant oscillation between activity and receptivity. How much better it is, I think, to be making frequent little movements between openness to the "one thing necessary" as represented by Mary and all the responsibilities of daily life as portrayed by Martha. Instead of trying to take great gulps and chunks of stillness and prayer, how much less stressful it is to intersperse the Office and lectio with smaller chunks, little breaths of quietness and openness to the Divine. How much more natural it is to allow that word or phrase that has caught my attention to reverberate in heart and mind and open me up to the eternity that beats beneath my conscious thought.

How much better it is to linger with the lilies for a few minutes, and then go on to what presents itself next, and then to linger again awhile later. Jesus knew so well that it is not good to build three booths and settle. We don't settle well; or rather, we settle all too well, and in the process we focus on whatever it is we're settling into—even the activity of prayer itself—and we lose the Spirit that infuses life and eternity into everything. For the Spirit only does so moment by moment.

It is indeed good to be here, and to linger. We very much need to linger. In our hyperactive culture we even need to remind ourselves that pausing is good. Yet, Jesus doesn't allow us to linger too long at a stretch. We linger only until the Spirit has moved us on.

abundance

It was the worst gardening year in memory. After a fairly normal spring, in mid-June the heavens opened and dropped down rain for weeks at a time. Bean and sunflower seeds, planted just before the deluge, rotted in the ground. Parsley took nearly a month to germinate. Tomatoes, peppers, eggplants, and melons, heat lovers all, sulked and refused to grow. The few days without rain were cloudy, cool, and humid. Nothing ever dried out.

Under these conditions, the shadow of blight grew ever larger and more menacing. Potatoes were stricken all over Maine, ours included. We yanked them out ruthlessly, so as not to spread the menace to other crops. I used copper spray, an organic fungicide, on the tomatoes and other nightshades, and even extended it to the basil. It fended off the blight, but the poor struggling plants urgently needed heat and sunlight, and there was precious little of either. Peaches are exceedingly marginal here in central Maine, so to have any crop at all is considered amazing. Yet, in the midst of this awful summer the trees were loaded with tiny green baby peaches. To get a good crop, they needed thinning. But I was busy, and besides, I didn't really believe they'd grow and ripen, so I ignored them.

Finally in mid-August we had a week of relative warmth and sun. By now those baby peaches were nearly full size. With sun and heat, they began to lose their greenness and turn that beautiful reddish yellow, which can only be called peach. In this worst of all years, was it possible that we were about to have a bumper crop of peaches?

Well, we did. They ripened slowly, over the course of about six weeks. First the Reliance tree, then the Red Haven—every single peach ripened. We picked bushels and bushels, all from only two trees. We gave them to our friends. We ate them daily. We froze them to make jam during the slow winter months. We gave bushels to a friend to make peach wine.

We marveled at the crop, and so did our friends. "Peaches in Maine," they all said. "Who would have believed it!"

Abundance of any sort seems downright unbelievable in an economy based on scarcity, on possessiveness, and on acquisition. Wikipedia, the online encyclopedia, tells us that "scarcity is the fundamental economic problem of having seemingly unlimited human needs and wants, in a world of limited resources. It states that society has insufficient productive resources to fulfill all human wants and needs. . . . Alternatively, scarcity implies that not all of society's goals can be pursued at the same time; trade-offs are made of one goal against others."[1]

That's a good, succinct statement of what seems to be the eternal human condition. We are made up of unlimited needs, wants, and desires, and there's simply not enough of anything to go around. I certainly wanted a productive garden, but that want was impossible to fulfill in this worst of all gardening years. I have many other needs and lots of wants and wishes, too. So does everyone else. We are all familiar with the gradual accumulation, over the years, of all the material goods we want or need, or think we want or need. Once upon a time, houses didn't even have closets. Now our supersized closets are stuffed to the brim, and we rent storage space to hold the overflow. We have yard sales, year after year, just to get rid of older items, to make room for new items. Many of these older items are not old or used at all. We acquired them, and then we didn't need them, or we forgot about them, or they weren't what we wanted after all. So out they go, and in comes some more, and in the process we never lose the hankering after more and more and more.

Worse, our economy seems to be built upon encouraging this tendency. Growth is everything, and consumption, we are told, drives this economic machine. Advertising drills into our heads the importance of owning everything we see, and even everything we imagine as well. Nowhere is there a suggestion that perhaps we already have enough, and maybe even more than enough.

So focused are we on wealth and acquisition, that we shiver at the thought of not having enough. We find it hard to imagine that someone might want less, not more. In such an intellectual and imaginative climate, our fears drive us to focus on the scarcity that seems to surround us. Abundance seems a mere dream, a chimera.

Yet, this is not the vision of the scriptures. In Genesis, we find ourselves set down in the midst of a garden, in which grew "every tree that is pleasant to the sight and good for food" (Gn 2:9). All of this was for free. The clear implication is that this garden, Eden, is a garden of abundance. Unfortunately, we got booted out of this garden of abundance into the mundane world of work and worry and scarcity. But the vision of abundance, and the hope for it, persisted. After the fall, and the tower, and the flood, and the call of Abraham, and Egypt, and the Passover, and the forty years in the desert, we find God eventually leading the Israelites into the Promised Land, the land "flowing with milk and honey." Surely that is an image of abundance!

But the Promised Land quickly lost its charm for the Chosen People, and time after time they abandoned the God who had given them so much. Eventually they lost the Promised Land, and were sent into exile. God sent prophets, who promised an eventual return, and new abundance. Isaiah sings of the promise of God: that God's people will be treated like an infant, nursing at God's abundant breasts, and that God will "extend prosperity to her like a river, and the wealth of the nations like an overflowing stream" (Gn 66:12).

In the New Testament, Jesus speaks of abundance, and he promises it. "Ask, and you shall receive," he says. "Seek, and you will find. Knock, and the door will be opened to you. For everyone who asks receives, and everyone who searches finds, and for everyone who knocks, the door will be opened. Is there anyone among you who, if your child asks for bread, will give a stone? . . . How much more will your Father in heaven give good things to those who ask him" (Mt 7:7–11).

Jesus offers a vision of the future. As in the Hebrew scriptures, it is a vision of an abundant banquet, rich in food, wine, friends, and joy. It is offered to everyone, and it is free. Like the peaches, ripening in rich abundance in the midst of a year of garden scarcity, it is the promise of rich abundance, above and beyond all our expectations.

Jesus not only promised this abundance for the future; he actually offered it to his followers in the midst of his teaching and travels. The multiplication of the loaves and fishes recounts his ability to provide plentiful nourishment for hordes of followers out of the scarcity of the deserted place. To make sure we get the point, the Gospels underline it for us: there were seven (or twelve, depending on the version) baskets full left over. Paradoxically, out of the dire scarcity of the moment, Jesus not only promises abundance; he provides it, and with plenty to spare.

The New Testament epistles are filled with images of abundance. But it is clearly not an abundance of material goods and wealth. Rather, this refers again and again to the abundance of God's

love and mercy, God's grace and glory. Paul's letter
to the Romans speaks of the "abundance of grace"
(Rom 5:17). In Philippians Paul speaks of the riches
of God's glory in Christ (see Phil 4:19). In Christ,
we are told, "all the fullness of God was pleased to
dwell"(Col 1:19), surely an image of the overflowing abundance found in God. Again, we read of
"Christ himself, in whom are hidden all the treasures of wisdom and knowledge"(Col 2:3). In these
instances, and throughout the Christian scriptures,
the many words and images of abundance refer not
to material wealth and plenty, but to the spiritual
realities promised and given by Jesus.

　　These earthen vessels, these bodies made of the
clay of the earth, these minds and psyches so filled
with wounds and emptiness, are so often oblivious
of the treasure they hold. We think of ourselves
sometimes as I thought of the weather that summer as "the most miserable garden year ever." Our
self-loathing sets itself up as a form of spirituality,
and encourages us to focus on all that is negative.
Yet, what is this treasure that we hold within? It
is nothing less than the Christ, "in whom all the
fullness of God was pleased to dwell"(Col 1:19). It
is an abundance of grace, the riches of God's glory,
mercy, and love. It is as though all this is shut up
within, and we don't even have the key. Worse,
we forget that we don't even need a key! It is as
though, in the midst of a miserable summer, we
cannot even look up at the tree and see those glorious, delicious peaches, waiting to be picked.

　　Jesus and the early evangelists focused our
attention on the abundance of God's gifts and

graces that fill us and surround us. Yet, our world continually reinforces the opposite image: that of scarcity. The world focuses our attention on all that we do not have. In doing so, it abets and increases our own woundedness and distrust, and these also concentrate on all we lack and want and think we need, yet don't have. Economics and our psyches, the external world and the internal, converge to bring us down and pull our attention away from all that is positive. We completely forget the treasure that is within, the giftedness that we have and are, and the abundance of gifts that surround us.

This focus on our poverty, both spiritual and material, is so misdirected. We think of abundance wrongly. We confuse it with material wealth. We also confuse it with freedom from the aching wound of unfulfilled want. Abundance is an attitude of heart, an openness to receive the gifts—the many, many gifts—that God gives us moment by moment. Most especially, it is the willingness to receive the most abundant gift of all: the indwelling of God's own self through the gift of the Spirit.

Perhaps abundance is more about gratitude and receptivity to the Spirit than about possessions and wealth. And gratitude and receptivity to God's Spirit are nearly always within our grasp. As an e-mail from an Orthodox monastery recently put it, "Abundance is a blessing, but *it is also a choice,* and not just dependent on outward circumstances."[2]

What a revolutionary way to think about abundance! It is a choice, not merely a condition over which we have little control. It is not dependent on having everything we want, whenever we want it. Nor is it dependent on our becoming at last the perfect person, never failing or at fault in anything. Rather, we are already gifted abundantly, here and now, not just in some future time—like the peaches, in the midst of the most miserable summer ever.

But how do we choose to live with an attitude of abundance? Perhaps, as that same e-mail suggests, it is through gratitude for all we are and have. Gratitude manifests itself in an attitude of thanksgiving in our prayer. Gratitude spills over into generosity, in our relationships with others. We can have material generosity, surely, in whatever way is open to us, and also generosity of heart: an attitude of openness, tolerance, patience, forbearance, kindness, forgiveness, and love toward others. Generosity of heart is an abundance of mind that is not quick to take offense but, rather, quick to forgive and overlook others' faults and failings. It is an abundance of heart that is open to receive what others have to say, even when we'd rather not hear it. It is an abundance of body that is unflagging in helpfulness to any who are in need, and yet is disciplined to hold back that helpfulness when others need to do things for themselves.

We have all been blessed in various ways. Some of us have been blessed with faith, some with our health, some with family or friends, and some with material goods. Most of all we are blessed with the abiding presence of God, who is with us in all things, guiding us from the Spirit within, and from the events and people around us. We have *all* been blessed in so many ways. Let us learn to share our gifts, and to shower this Spirit generously on all whom we meet. If we do this, then, as Jesus says, "A good measure, pressed down, shaken together, running over, will be put into your lap" (Lk 6:38).

autumn

goldenrod days

Today is September 1, and for the last few weeks I have been enjoying the sight of goldenrod blooming outside my window. These ubiquitous but lovely wildflowers are not growing in the cloister garden, though I could well plant them there. Rather, I admire them where they grow wild outside of the east window of my cell.

East of the row of cells, we have a narrow strip of lawn, which ends in a perennial border in front of an old, tumbledown stone wall. This wall extends along the entire row of hermitage cells, continuing into the woods to the north. It is bisected by an old tote road—now our prayer trail—immediately south of the hermitage, and then the wall continues south beyond the tote road. In front of this wall, facing the cells, I am slowly planting a perennial border. Beyond it the hill falls away to the east in overgrown pasture and blueberry fields. Down in the valley the trees begin. The forest continues as far as I can see across a broad, uninhabited valley. Far away, perhaps as much as ten or twelve miles, a range of hills rises to the east. They, too, are wooded, though there are patches of lighter green on them that indicate pasture or blueberry fields or hayfields. A line of high-tension electric wires extends up and over the largest of the hills.

The perennial border is still new and unfinished. To plant it, I've had to excavate the top several inches of soil and replace it with topsoil. It's hard work, and I can only squeeze it in by stealing time from other tasks. I grumble as I do it, for it seems so unnecessary. The excavator who backfilled when we built the hermitage did so with sand instead of topsoil. But not much will grow in six inches of sand, so I must work to correct this major error.

I've begun from both ends of the border, and the perennials do well, though not as well as I could wish. Some sand remains beneath them, and they get full sun and lots of wind, so they dry out easily in spite of all the mulch I've used. I haven't yet worked on the center of the border, which is still a wasteland of sand and weeds. On top of it, a different and far more knowledgeable excavator left a load of topsoil for me to use after I've taken out the sand. This heap of topsoil has sprouted all sorts of plants, including some spectacular goldenrod. For the last several weeks I've enjoyed watching it come into bloom.

Many years ago I noticed that goldenrod begins blooming earlier here in Maine than in southern New England, where I grew up. Then I began to notice that there are many different kinds of goldenrod. This year, as I watch the show unfolding outside my window, I've become aware that different kinds bloom at different times. The first kind, which I think is called Sweet Goldenrod, began turning golden in early August. Gradually, I noticed a larger kind to its left and slightly behind it but not yet in bloom. Over the last week Sweet Goldenrod has slowly begun fading and turning gray, while at the same time, this other kind—perhaps it is Stiff Goldenrod, though I'm not at all sure—has begun turning golden. It is my own lovely, personal show of the ripening of summer as it dwindles into autumn.

It's a wonderful thing to watch this golden glory against the backdrop of the blue hills as I sit in my cell for prayer and lectio—that is, the slow, prayerful reading of a spiritual book. In mornings, I am up long before Vigils and sip my coffee as I watch dawn break and the day lighten. Sunup comes at about the beginning of Vigils these days, so after it I sit in my chair with my book for lectio and gaze out over the valley, letting the delicious emptiness and quiet of this beautiful space and this lovely morning fill my heart. We have been blessed with glorious weather these last few weeks: golden, late-summer, early-fall weather, when Maine is imbued with a foretaste of paradise. Or is it Eden? Or maybe both. These are days of sun and warmth, with blue, blue skies, low humidity, and

a delectable breeze. I sit here and think that surely
this is what heaven must be about. There is a wonderful Latin chant, "Salve Festa Dies," about the joy
and glory of Easter, the greatest feast of the Church
year. To me it echoes what must be the delight and
peace of heaven—all with a lovely depth of prayerful tranquility.

> Salve festa dies toto venerabilis aevo
> > Qua deus infernum vicit
> > Et astra tenet.
> Ecce renascentis testator gratia mundi
> > Omnia cum Domino dona redisse suo.

> Hail, festive day, forever revered,
> > On which God conquered hell
> > And held sway over the stars.
> Look, the earth, born again, shows thanks
> > By rendering unto her Lord all her gifts.[1]

"The earth . . . shows thanks by rendering
unto her Lord all her gifts." These words could
surely be written about late summer, on the cusp
of autumn. The garden overflows with produce:
tomatoes, beans, eggplant, peppers, melons, chard,
onions, cabbage. We have been gathering delicious
peaches for the first time from our young trees.
Apples are ripening on the old trees at the south
end of the stone wall. Blackberries are lush down
by the prayer trail. The gifts of earth's abundance,
freely given, are surely a foretaste of the messianic
banquet of heaven.

And the space, the stillness, the silence! There
is a tradition, still alive and well, at least among

the Orthodox Churches, called *hesychia*. It means "stillness." Early mornings and evenings here, with the goldenrod and the hills and the sky, seem to be clasped in the embrace of stillness. Hesychia. Golden days, stillness, gratitude. "The earth, born again, shows thanks by rendering unto her Lord all her gifts." And I, born anew each time I enter into this blessed stillness, this delicious emptiness, am filled with gratitude.

Yet, hesychia, stillness, is not primarily about exterior stillness, precious though that might be. *Hesychia* is about the stillness of the heart. After days of blessed emptiness, peace, stillness, and gratitude, this morning the stillness surrounds my heavy heart but does not enter. Today I look out, and the gold seems gray. The day is perfect, but I am not. Today stillness is outside, but not within. Nor can I recapture it at will.

This morning I woke up to sadness. It does not spring from these golden days or from the events of these days. It comes from old times, from reminiscences of various earlier traumas. Not that I have been remembering such things lately—my life has been too full and rich for that. But this sacred stillness has a way of moving us beyond all the layers of self-protection and self-oblivion, a way of bringing us deep into our hearts, deep down to where we are all still children.

I pick up John Cassian, the fifth-century monastic author, for he has a chapter on sadness. It's a short chapter, yet he packs a lot into it. He speaks of two kinds of sadness. One is a sadness that leads to God. This sadness is compounded by regret for past misdeeds and desire for the peace and joy of God's blessed kingdom, both present and future.

This sadness I experience is not of God, I am sure; for here I sit surrounded by tokens of present blessings and images of blessings still to be, and yet I remain unmoved. Rather, this "consuming sadness" of which Cassian speaks is of another sort. He lists its symptoms: "It cuts us off totally from the vision of divine contemplation and weakens and oppresses the mind itself. . . . It does not carry out its prayers . . . nor dwell upon the remedies of the sacred readings. It does not suffer it to be peaceable and gentle with the brothers [or sisters], makes it impatient and abrupt with regard to every duty of work and worship."[2] This could have been written for me.

Where does this sadness come from? Cassian gives several possibilities. One is the sadness that often follows anger. Another possibility is that our desire for something, however great or trivial, has not been fulfilled. We want something and we don't get it, so we are dejected. The third possibility is mysterious: there is no easily discernible reason. Though our current understanding of depression was unknown in Cassian's day, he undoubtedly describes it here.

Cassian gives a list of remedies for this sadness—though none of them will fully work for what we now know as depression. Today we know the importance of diagnosis and medication for this widespread disease. Yet, the value of holding fast to hope and faith in something greater than ourselves should not be underestimated.

However, this sadness of mine is not depression, at least not yet. It could turn into depression if it were to continue for very long. But I have discovered another remedy over the years, another way of encountering this sadness.

Slowly, very slowly, I have learned not to run from it, not to defend myself from it—but rather, to embrace it. Stillness has brought me into my heart, and in my heart—as in each person's heart—dwells a loving, helpless, vulnerable child. A beautiful child. In my case this morning, she is a child filled with sadness. Slowly I have learned to encircle this beautiful, fragile, vulnerable, sad child with my loving adult arms of compassion and gentleness. Slowly I have learned to treasure this little child. Slowly I have learned to let her sadness have its time and place in the sunshine of my adult love, a pale but real reflection of God's love.

Amazingly, when I can remember to do this, I discover anew that at the heart of this child is someone else. Perhaps I should say: *Someone Else.* At the heart of this child, I discover the heart of God, the heart of Jesus, who was also the vulnerable, loving One and who allowed himself to experience our vulnerability, our helplessness. The child Jesus wanted to be close to other children. This child close to the child in my heart, at your heart, is the Christ Child: the vulnerable, loving, beautiful One.

Isabel Allende, speaking about her book *The Sum of Our Days*, has this to say: "I don't want to get rid of that sadness; it's part of who I am today. I feel like it's a fertile soil at the bottom of my heart where everything wonderful grows—creativity, compassion, love, and even joy."[3]

In the midst of beauty, stillness, and hesychia arose the turbulence of sadness. And yet, embracing this sorrow has brought me even deeper, to a deeper stillness, a stillness "at the still point of the turning world," as T. S. Eliot said. That ancient chant "Salve Festa Dies" continues to hold meaning today. "Hail, festive day . . . on which God conquered hell and held sway over the stars." The route to stillness, to peace, to the heart of life, and to heaven as well, lies through darkness, through sadness, through heaviness.

Goldenrod days, moments of timelessness, have brought me to my heart.

diminishment

"Be all you can be," urges a classic ad for the Army. It clearly implies that being more and better is what we "can be": better, greater, more productive, more wealthy, more famous, more important. We are continually urged to strive toward all of these values, not only in the obvious way of this ad, but in ceaseless subliminal ways by our contacts, our culture, and our society's goals and symbols.

"He must increase, but I must decrease," said John the Baptist (Jn 3:30). A famous saying, it was made more famous by the horrific mode of John's diminishment. Diminishment, we feel, must of necessity be awful. It is made to seem still more awful because it runs completely counter to our cultural models of importance.

Nor does one need to be literally cut off in the midst of life for us to feel this way. We witness with silent panic the parade of our elders—stooping, diminishing, fading away before our very eyes—knowing we are helpless to stop or even slow the process.

We know, and we resist knowing, that this is our future as well. How we resist this knowledge! We hide it away, ignoring it, focusing on youth and beauty and health. We keep in shape, honing our minds, and doing all we can to remain in control. Yet, aging and diminishment cannot ultimately be controlled. Nor, for that matter, can life.

It's hard to let go. It's both hard to let go of something we love, and nearly as hard to let go of something we're merely used to. It's hard to let go of the old, familiar ways and to open ourselves to the new. Usually we do so only under pressure of necessity.

Yes, it's hard to let go of something we love. Gardening may not be my vocation, but nonetheless, I love it. It brings me into intimate contact with God's creation. It keeps my muscles and joints and lungs healthy. It gives us fresh, healthy vegetables for our table and beautiful flowers for our chapel— not to mention the beauty of the grounds where they grow. Yet, in spite of all these blessings, the gardens came to be a major problem, for there are too many of them.

Slowly, over the years, the gardens have grown in size and number. First, there were the cloister gardens, which were four huge raised beds. At least these were contained. Then, to put beauty and order where chaos reigned, outside of our cells, I gradually added the stone-wall border. Next we built a guest house, and once we cleared ground for it, there was another blank space, so another garden went in. And the kitchen garden also grew, so that it would be large enough to sustain a four-year crop rotation. Finally, as the guest house neared completion, another garden was planted behind it, a lovely perennial border with stone steps leading to the field and the apple trees. This one is overlooked by the guest rooms, to provide a serene and inviting space for those here on retreat.

So, little by little, the gardens have grown, and always for a good reason. But the result is that now they are too much, and they need to diminish. A year ago I began work to downsize the great raised beds in the cloister. They were enormous: twelve by fifteen feet each. Since they'd been in place for five years, the perennials in them were also enormous. I began by dividing plants and giving them away. Then I began the laborious process of removing a foot of topsoil from about half of the square footage. The beds are now half the size they once were—and they are still too large.

In my checkup last winter, the doctor strongly warned me that I needed to lose weight. It's something I'd known for years, and somehow always avoided. It was never the right time: there was too much happening, or I was struggling with other issues, or I couldn't face another challenge—there was always a reason not to face this simple physical diminishment. But now, finally, it was time. The doctor told me this, but also my body was telling me by means of a variety of aches and pains, through lack of energy and through fatigue, through high cholesterol and elevated blood sugar.

So now it was time. But it's hard to let go of something you love—as I love and enjoy food.

"Our limits are the outline of our vocation," said spiritual theologian Adrian Van Kamm.[1] When I heard this recently, it came as affirmation. Here indeed is the response to the "be all you can be" generation. As children, we were told that in America anyone can grow up to be president. Perhaps this is so for exceedingly exceptional persons, but for most of us, as adults, our rational minds tell us this is not true; yet subliminally, unconsciously, that ambitious message is retained. Each time we suffer diminishment, we find ourselves lost, bereaved, cheated, perhaps even bitter. This is the land of opportunity, is it not? So why should we not be able to be all we can be, all the time, every day? The bitter acknowledgment of limits all too often means for us the loss of dreams and the death of hope.

As for myself, I came to Maine in my early thirties, as I always say, "kicking and screaming." It was six years before I was able to finally accept this seemingly horrific diminishment. Maine, as a friend once said, is literally at "the end of the extension cord" in terms of worldly careers, accomplishments, or powerful places to be. "This is Siberia, Lord," I cried.

This is exile, I told myself over and over and over. At the time, of course, and for many years since, I failed to appreciate that all of our life on earth is an exile from our true homeland in God's kingdom. Like the Israelites in the desert, we are on pilgrimage, journeying through the desert of this life toward the Promised Land. But at age thirty, with my college friends and religious colleagues making great strides in careers and vocations, I didn't see it that way. All I could see was that I was stuck here in Maine, away from everything that I believed to be important and necessary.

Even now, today, as I sit here scribbling away, pen in hand, yellow pad on knee, on a bench in a park overlooking Penobscot Bay—with large pines towering over me, thunderhead cumulus clouds riding low to the east, bits of scraggly goldenrod, stunted firs, and a great decayed stump riddled with ant holes and covered with lichens and reindeer moss; with the tide flowing blue and rippling calmly toward the seaweed-covered rocks; and with kayakers calling to one another as they paddle down the bay—even today I must accept my woeful inability to convey the beauty and peace and invisible currents of love and longing stretching out, weaving across the blue, blue water and around the hazy distant islands between me and the transcendent One and back again. I can only know—having learned piecemeal, slowly—that my limitations and my diminishment, my exile here in Maine, are what have made me whole. Even more, they are used by God as a vehicle for—who knows?—you, perhaps, reading this someday, somewhere, in a foreign land and as an exile yourself.

My limits have been the outline, the contours, the profile of my vocation. As a child I was always the bright one, the one of whom great things were expected. In my teen years, I read about St. Teresa of Avila and fell in love with the idea of myself as a great mystic. Later I dreamed of entering Carmel

—and, no doubt, soon being elected prioress. But fortunately God knew my limits far better than I, and let me know, clearly, beyond doubt, that I was meant to be in Maine, in spite of my dread and fear. It took six long, painful years to recognize and accept this reality, and it has taken many more years to see the utter rightness of it. The bright child, in love with mysticism, has had to come to terms with her own realities: her poverty, her fearfulness, her lack of powerful connections, her shyness, her arrogance, her inability to roll with the punches life can often throw. All these limits have formed the outline that God has used to fashion my very unique, very particular, very personal vocation. From all these inabilities, these lacks, these holes, God has forged a call, which uses these very limits to form my vocation.

"By restraint we are made whole," says Wendell Berry.[2] If he is right, and I believe he is, then restraint, the gracious acceptance of our limits, even of our diminishment, enables us to find our own unique place on earth. This unique place may include our physical dwelling, our true life's work, our mind's enlightenment, our heart's liberation and love and contentment. My own diminishment, my seemingly God-imposed exile to the desert of Maine, has over the years become my true home and the source of rich and fruitful new life.

"He must increase, but I must decrease." This is as true for us today as ever it was for John the Baptist. We take that as loss, yet it is supreme gift of life.

Take another saying from the Gospels. "What is the kingdom of God like? To what shall I compare it? It is like a mustard seed that someone took and sowed in the garden; it is the smallest of all seeds but when it has grown it is the greatest of shrubs and becomes a tree, and the birds of the air made nests in its branches." And again, "It is like yeast that a woman took and mixed in with three measures of flour until all of it was leavened" (Lk 13:18–19, 21). The tiny mustard seed, the leaven, the pearl of great price, the lost coin—these are the images Jesus uses to describe the kingdom. But they are all tiny! Capable of giving life, no doubt, they are yet so tiny, so inconsequential—at least to the eye of one who only looks for the large, the glorious, the outwardly productive, the spectacular. Our vaulting ambitions, our glorious dreams and even more glorious daydreams—do they not turn our attention, our focus, our heart's longings, to ephemeral and even nonexistent realities? Paradoxically, it is in accepting our own limitations, the realities of our own physical, emotional, and environmental conditions, and through working with the diminished capacities that we actually have, that we are enlarged and empowered by God's Spirit into the fullness of life.

As I write this in late summer, the garden has never looked so lovely—in spite of a summer of dismal weather. Two guinea fowl appeared mysteriously soon after the arrival of the Japanese beetles, took up residence under the raspberries, and proceeded to devour the beetles by the hundreds and thousands. They remained long enough to save our raspberry crop and then, just as mysteriously, they disappeared. No doubt they were merely following their own particular food chain, but I can't help see it as an example of God's unfathomable providence affirming my decision to restrain my desire for more beauty and to downsize the garden to manageable proportions.

The guinea fowl helped save the roses as well. Roses, daylilies, Oriental lilies and Echinacea flourished and bloomed; and the garden, though smaller, looked lovelier than ever. Perhaps because it is smaller, and more manageable, I am able to tend it more carefully. The plants reward me by flourishing. In fact they flourish so well that I find I need to prune them often. I am reminded of another scriptural metaphor: "I am the true vine," Jesus tells us. "My Father is the vinegrower. Every branch that bears fruit he prunes to make it bear more fruit"(Jn 15:1, 2b). It seems counterintuitive, yet every gardener knows the truth of this saying. Now that the raspberries have finished bearing, I need to prune them, because if I don't, the plants will be weakened, and next year's crop will be less. Pruning them now will produce a flourishing crop next year. Diminishment, even with raspberries, even with grapes and apples and pears and peaches, is a good thing. Diminishment, restraint, limitations, even with people, even with myself, is a very good thing.

And what about weight loss, which aims at a specific kind of physical diminishment, and is the fruit of a particular kind of restraint? Now that I am many pounds lighter, I find my energy has doubled. I sleep beautifully, as I did when I was young. I can garden all day long—when I can find the time to do so! I no longer puff or stop to rest when I'm coming up that long, steep hill on the prayer trail. This is a diminishment that has paid immediate and obvious rewards.

"He must increase, but I must decrease." But who is it that increases, when I accept my diminishment, and willingly decrease? It is the one who set us the example of willing diminishment, the one who, "though he was in the form of God, did not regard equality with God as something to be exploited, but emptied himself, taking the form of a slave, being born in human likeness, he humbled himself and became obedient to the point of death—even death on a cross" (Phil 2:6–8). The Word of God willingly accepted his own diminishment in order to enter into humanity and redeem us. Our own acceptance of limitations and diminishment allows the entrance of God's Spirit—the Spirit of Jesus—to take root and grow and bloom in us. "Our vocation is to be Jesus, and Jesus is to live in us," said Mother Aloysius, a twentieth-century Carmelite from Concord, New Hampshire.

We are each called to witness to God's kingdom by living out our own particular and unique facet of the jewel that is God. How amazing! By surrendering ourselves to this process of diminishment, we are actually enlarged into God's very life and being and presence. We lose the false trappings, the needs and desires and compulsions that bind us to the passing convulsions of this world, and we find our true vocation, our true calling in God. In doing so, we are empowered to become God's redemptive presence in this hurting, wounded, bleeding world: a presence of mercy and peace, justice and strength, freedom and joy.

Not that this is an easy process! Nor is it ever completed either—not until at last we, too, enter into aging and death. We do not choose the diminishment of death, yet it will come for each one of us. For some it comes early, for some late. We can practice getting ready for it throughout our lives, as we accept and embrace all the little diminishments that happen to us along the way. We can fight it, as I fought the diminishment of living in Maine. Or we can embrace it, surrender to it, and discover the hidden life it holds within.

As I sat on that park bench overlooking Penobscot Bay on that late summer afternoon, furiously scribbling away, I heard a group approaching on the path. One of them sounded loud and obnoxious. I hoped they would hurry past me. As they emerged into the clearing, I realized that the loud one, who was in the rear, was actually a teenager and also mentally disabled. As they crossed in front of me, she turned, looked at me directly, and asked, "Are you an author?" An *author!* I'd never been addressed this way before! Emotion surged up within as I realized that this unlettered and clearly disabled young woman had recognized me—had even recognized this emergent new vocation of writing. *An author!* I missed a beat, just half a beat, and then said, acknowledging it myself for the first time, "Yes, I am." And then she was past.

But as they walked on, the woman ahead of her, clearly her mom, called back to me and said, "She has a friend in a learning group who writes. You can see she is an exceptional child." And as they entered the woods ahead, continuing along their own path, I responded.

"Yes," I said, "I can see."

approaching darkness

Since late June the days have been growing shorter. Imperceptibly at first, by September it is very noticeable. Sunset is markedly earlier, sunrise later. Compline is now sung after dark, while during summer it was still full day. The shadow of the building creeps farther north across the cloister garden; it falls sooner and lingers longer. Where once I had afternoon sunlight in my cell, now it is in shadow. Plants in the two raised beds that get the most shade grow tall and leggy, straining for the sun. The shadow of the cell wing falls across the perennial border earlier each day, and by mid-October the end of Vespers finds us already in dusk.

It is markedly colder as well. By late August, a sweater is sometimes helpful in the evening; in September it's a necessity. While there are still mild days, the weather is often chill, windy, and raw, particularly in a September rainstorm. October can bestow upon us the caress of Indian summer, but it can equally present us with a glancing foretaste of winter.

Last night we finally had our first killing frost. For most people it arrived earlier, but we are on top of the hill, and frost flows downward, so we escaped—that is, until last night. This morning, the garden is dead. Leaves are blackened; stalks stand stiff, shorn of greenery. The last of the sunflowers hang their great heads down, heavy with seed, the blossoms killed. Bruised and grubby leaves reflect the darkness that advances. Despite sunshine and clean, crisp air, death and darkness are a present reality in the garden this morning.

Ironically, many people (myself included) will tell you that autumn is their favorite time of year. It is a lovely time: spectacular autumn foliage; clear, crisp days; mild afternoons; apples and cider; the end of mosquitoes and bugs. Autumn is undeniably beautiful, but it also holds a foretaste of darkness and chill. The leaves are falling, frost is killing the gardens, vegetation is rotting, and the year is coming to an end. All this whispers to us that, someday, our end will come also. Our night is approaching.

When I was young, all of this was overlaid by the beauty of the season, and by youth. Fall was not the time of endings, but of beginnings. Always, autumn meant a new school year! Whether studying or teaching, it was another beginning. One year in midlife it changed. One year, suddenly, darkness approached. On a beautiful, clear, crisp early-autumn day, sadness opened up within, and my understanding of autumn—and of life—forever changed.

Perhaps this happens, in one way or another, for most of us. In youth, we feel invincible, immortal. But time progresses inexorably, one year after another. At some point, we begin to notice the accumulation of years. Our bodies slow down a bit; we begin to wonder if we can really accomplish all our hopes and dreams. We notice our limitations, and we also notice that people get ill, that people even die.

The early monastics understood that death and darkness is an ever-present reality. No doubt they lived more closely with these harsher realities of life. No doubt today we attempt to insulate ourselves from illness, despair, and death. Yet, still these creep in. We see them on TV; we feel their cool breath on our necks when a loved one becomes ill. They seep into our dreams at night, our anxieties and phobias by day.

As believers, we look to our faith to help us deal with this; as Christians, we look to the Cross. We believe in the Resurrection, we believe in Easter, and we believe in life without end. Yet, when darkness envelops us, such glorious realities can seem far, far away. How is it possible to live out of our faith, when darkness surrounds us, when we seem to live and move in the midst of a dense fog? What can penetrate the cold that has permeated our lives?

Some time ago I read a book called *The Life of Moses*. Written in the fourth century, by the brilliant

and creative spiritual theologian St. Gregory of
Nyssa, it describes the journey of Moses, who led
the Hebrew people out of Egypt and through the
desert, until they were within sight of the Promised
Land. Gregory observes that Moses is not only a
forerunner and prototype of Jesus, but also a forerunner and prototype of each and every believing
Christian. Gregory has profound insight into the
life of Moses—and of each one of us. He noticed
that as Moses progressed in his life, leading the
Israelites out of Egypt and into the desert, Moses
followed God in a pillar of cloud. And as he progressed even farther, going to meet God on the
mountain, he entered into thick darkness. Yet,
Gregory does not see these as negative things, nor
does he particularly refer them to the Cross.

Rather, for Gregory, this journey into fog and
darkness is the *normal* progression of the spiritual
journey. Gregory's approach to darkness is positive. Rather than signs of decay and death, these
are signs of life and health. Gregory believes that
our initial journey with the Lord takes place with
a great burst of light and understanding. This happens, for instance, at a time of conversion, a sudden moment of deepening faith and insight. Or it
can happen that we grow in enlightenment as we
struggle to move away from our habitual faults
and failings. To do this is to walk in light. When we
walk in light, the divine image which has been lost
through sin becomes restored in us.

Incontestably this was true for me as a young
adult and a new Christian and Catholic. Everything, it seemed, was radiant with light. How clear

it all seemed! In a way, I liken it to springtime in the garden. I have such great plans! I can envision my garden so clearly! Even the earth, newly tilled, its clean, bare earth beckoning, makes everything look so clear, so uncomplicated.

Yet, time continues its inexorable progression, and spring becomes summer. Weeds spring up. There is not enough rain. Or there is too much rain, and at the wrong time. Perhaps there's not enough calcium in the soil, and so the tomatoes get blossom end rot. Or a wilt attacks my basil. What did I do wrong? Could I have done something different? Oh, it has all gone amiss, and it is so puzzling.

Our lives can be like that difficult, unruly garden, in the midst of a stretch of uncontrollable, miserable weather. Life can become very complicated. As a young adult I thought I had tried my best to follow the Lord, but ended up at a dead end. I asked to speak to a priest I knew who was a well-respected author and spiritual father. As we began, I simply didn't know what to say, and so I blurted out what welled up from within, "I just feel so very lost." I will never forget the utter calm and placidity with which he replied, "That's because you're living a spiritual life, sister. If you thought you knew exactly where you are, I would worry about you. The fact that you're so lost only means that God is in charge, not yourself."

My friend was speaking out of a profound understanding that to move along on the spiritual journey is to move, like Moses, into the fog and into darkness. Like Gregory of Nyssa, like Moses, he understood that life gets complicated. In fact, it

gets cloudy, murky, difficult. Our daily lives can
be filled with the fog of obscurity. In that fog, we
need to look and listen deeply for the inner, spiritual meaning of things. We need to pay attention
to the details, for God's will and loving presence
are often revealed in the smallest of things. God
has long ago got our attention in that first burst
of brilliant clarity. Now we are deep in the journey, and we've become accustomed to the light—
so accustomed that perhaps we've forgotten how
much light we actually have. Now we need to pay
attention differently. We are in the cloud, and darkness is approaching. No need to panic, we need
merely to refine our focus.

A friend of mine pointed out that when we're
driving in fog, we don't want to use our bright
lights, since these would simply reflect the fog into
our eyes and blind us. No, we need to use low light,
focused down on the bit of road that's close in front
of us. In fog we can't see the far horizon; we must
pay close attention to the path that is only one step
ahead. That's true in the fog of our lives as well, as
we learn to trust that God will give us the guidance
to see that next step. We aren't given a clear understanding of the entire journey; we are only given
the next step. And so we learn to lean on God in all
the little details of life.

> Moses and Aaron were among his priests,
> Samuel also was among those
> who called on his name.
> They cried to the Lord, and he answered them.
> He spoke to them in the pillar of cloud. (Ps 99:6–7a)

Perhaps we're having a difficulty with a family member or friend and are not sure how to handle it. We need to trust that God will give us the insight we need and that God will continue to lead us in the midst of this conflict—even in the midst of our own uncertainty.

Not sure where we're going in life? Not sure of our direction? We take the next step indicated, not knowing where it will lead, and move deeper into trust. To do this, we need our fog lights: those low-down, close-up beams that seek out and learn from the little details of the situation.

In the garden in a difficult summer, I need to pay attention to lots of factors to learn what's going on, and what I need to do to help the plants to thrive. So in my own life, in the midst of fog and darkness, I need to refocus and pay attention. As Gregory notes, "In this crossing [of the Red Sea] the cloud served as guide. Those before us interpreted the cloud well as the grace of the Holy Spirit, who guides toward the Good those who are worthy. Whoever follows him passes through the water, since the guide makes a way through it for him. In this way, he is safely led to freedom."[1]

Can it get any worse than this thick, blinding fog? Indeed it can! As the autumn darkness grows and the light ebbs, so in our lives, darkness can also grow. Who are we? What are we doing with our lives? Have we made the right decisions long ago, or was it all a mistake? These and similar questions can take possession of us and fill our hearts with darkness. Autumn is beautiful, but it is often the time when we begin to hear intimations of our own limitations and mortality. Darkness approaches.

As Gregory of Nyssa knew, this darkness is an invitation from the Lord, not necessarily to suffering and cross, but to a deeper life of faith—or perhaps even to a relationship with the Lord that is of a different sort. As darkness deepens, we are invited to embrace it as *gift*, even as a very special gift. "Clouds and thick darkness are all around him" (Ps 97:2). Gregory knew that cloud and darkness can be the greatest of gifts, even the gift of seeing God: "The contemplation of God is not effected by sight and hearing, nor is it comprehended by any of the customary perceptions of the mind. For *no eye has seen, and no ear has heard,* nor does it belong to those things which usually enter *into the heart of man.*"[2]

If we cannot see or hear God, if he is beyond all human comprehension and knowledge, how can we come to know him? Why are we given this desire to see him, if it is truly impossible? Gregory tells us: "When, therefore, Moses grew in knowledge, he declared that he had seen God in the darkness." What God? "He who *made darkness his hiding place.*"[3]

Darkness is God's hiding place? How very strange. And yet, I remember, on that same lovely autumn day when darkness opened up before me and my world shuddered, that it was a new beginning, a new walk with the Lord. It was a walk into deep blindness, into what seemed the very heart of darkness. I learned to pay attention to all that happened, both within and without. And in the midst of the gloom, I slowly became aware of God's peaceful, calm, placid presence—God's abundantly loving presence. Darkness has slowed me down and changed my focus. It was merely the outer covering of God's loving presence.

> He made darkness his covering around him, his canopy thick clouds dark with water. Out of the brightness before him there broke through his clouds hailstones and coals of fire. (Ps 18:11–12)

Darkness does indeed approach in this autumn. The nights grow longer; the cold deepens. Outside the cloister, in the world at large, turmoil increases. Within my heart, I feel the cloud of numerous conflicts and questions. Yet, these ominous shadows, filled as they are with ambiguities, conflicts, questions, and fear, hold a warm and living secret, if I can but embrace it. Darkness approaches to open me up to a God who is beyond my clarity, beyond my expectations, beyond my desires, certainly beyond all my fears and doubts and difficulties. These will remain; the black cloud does not make them go away. Yet, in the obscurity that approaches, if I pay close attention, I find the glowing and loving heart of the incomprehensible God who is with me in the midst of it. Darkness approaches, but it is luminous with God.

true colors

As I dig onions out of the cool, wet earth, my fingers thickly crusted and oozing with mud, summer seems to close down behind me, and winter's cool breath hovers. Pulling onions, digging potatoes, cleaning out the garden—these end of season tasks are no less pleasurable for being messy. The garden in autumn is always raggedy and unkempt, and yet I always love it. This year it's untidy, muddy, and overgrown—yet filled with disheveled appeal.

The vegetable garden has a few perennials as well, many of them autumn bloomers. As I squelch through the onion patch, I find myself working right alongside some towering asters, one of bright pink and one a deep, blueish purple. Behind them is an enormous clump of *miscanthus*, a great circle of plant material, two feet in diameter and more

191

than six feet high, with lovely soft, waving plumes
of white seed head. Their long, slender, gracefully
trailing leaves are turning all sorts of marvelous
shades of bronze and russet and tan.

The garden is not alone in proclaiming the
beauty of autumn. This clear, cool day, the stiff-
ening winds that speed yesterday's storm on its
way down east—all seems meant to highlight the
dazzling colors of autumn foliage. Maples and
ash lining the stone wall flaunt their red and gold
with fiery abandon. Ash and red maple are the
first to turn; later come the sugar maples in glorious orange and golden display. Next are the birch
and poplar and beech, a bit more subdued but still
glowing, and last the oaks, in shades of bronze and
rust and gold, more subtle but no less beautiful.
Just as in spring, with the display of baby leaves
and unobtrusive flowers, so in autumn each species
has its own loveliness, its own special qualities, and
its own timing. Indeed, each tree seems to have its
own particular shade of glory, affected a bit each
year by the weather, but nonetheless true to its own
distinct version of dying splendor.

Scientists tell us that the glorious colors of
autumn leaves are actually their true colors. The
greens of spring and summer are only a mask,
caused by the presence of chlorophyll in the leaves,
which is needed to carry out the photosynthesis
that provides the miraculous task of turning sunlight and carbon dioxide into food. Photosynthesis
is an amazing alchemy, the source of life here on
earth, providing the basic food necessary for all
life to exist.

But as the nights lengthen and days shorten, trees begin to shut down for the winter. Their chlorophyll breaks down, allowing the pigments of yellow and gold to appear. Yet another pigment shows forth as reds and purples. This can combine with the yellows to produce orange. Put all this together, and *voila!* we have the spectacular display of autumn.

Autumnal display and cooling earth always seems to signal something more as well for myself: an urge, not exactly melancholy, but reflective. The earth and trees begin to turn inward, and so do I. The busy fruitfulness of summer is done, this final blaze of glory passes swiftly, and then the long, slow death of winter lives for months. The journey takes another turn.

How marvelous it is that green leaves on trees are camouflage, smoke screens, almost a kind of falsity; and only at journey's end do leaves reveal their true colors. There are messages here for me: images of the human journey, a journey so filled and overfilled with images and masks and personas—sometimes suited to us, often outgrown and discarded, but never perfectly who we really are.

Are these dazzling colors a visual image of who I am called to be? Do they impart some reminiscence of my immortal soul, as it came from the hand of its Creator? Perhaps.

Spirituality is filled with stories of masks and smoke screens, guidance on how to overcome them, visions of the glory lying behind them, and rules on how to get there. I should know: I've spoken of this myself, talked about it, taught it, worked on it

in myself and in others. The false self is a term that
expresses an important contemporary understanding of who we are in this life, and how this covers
over our real self, our true self, created in God's
image and called to live out that image. To be blunt:
green leaves are the false self, the layers and layers
of mask and protection that have built up around
our true self, like the layers of these onions I'm so
industriously harvesting. The autumnal blaze of
glory is the image of God in us, our true self.

Many and varied are the ways in which this
false-self/true-self dichotomy is described. Some
call it "identity." Some call it "self." Some call it
"soul." No matter the description, the mask is
always a given, as is the long and arduous journey
to the dazzle, a fitting reality for which the annual
cycle of trees and leaves is the external shadow.

"I came into the world with a false self. I was
born in a mask. I came into existence under a sign
of contradiction, being someone that I was never
intended to be and therefore a denial of what I am
supposed to be. And thus I came into existence and
nonexistence at the same time because from the
very start I was something that I was not."[1] This is
Thomas Merton, equating the false self with sin—
not the grubby sins, large or small, that we all spend
our lives falling into or else evading. Rather, like the
greenness of the leaves, it's a condition in which we
find ourselves, a stuckness at the heart of life. It's
an attitude, perhaps, of possessiveness, graspiness,
with ourselves at the center of everything. It is an
ontological fault line, debris of Adam's fall.

Thus we are all embedded in the false self. The story line of our lives aims at disentangling ourselves from this web and stepping into the freedom of the true self. Paradox lurks, however. The ego cannot disentangle itself. All plans, all actions, all rules, can of themselves only deepen the ego's control. Work, and plan, and pray—and await deliverance.

This is the contemporary model: analytic, psychological, intellectualist. The ancient version is not a model, but a collection of images sketched out over a dozen centuries and thousands of lives; and it comes from the Hebrew scriptures. It's not about the self here; it's about the heart. In the Old Testament, the heart is the core of the human person, the center of the conscious human personality. It is the source of human emotion as well, not the superficial, sentimental emotion of the Valentine hearts and flowers or a Hallmark card. Yes, the heart is the source of emotions, but not the maudlin kind.

But the early Hebrews understood that the heart is also the source of desire and will. It is the place of decision. Proverbs says, "Keep your heart with all vigilance" (Prv 4:23). And in Psalm 95 we read, "O that today you would listen to his voice! Do not harden your hearts" (Ps 95:7b–8a). Hearing and obedient response are meant to go together: we hear with the ear of our heart, and we respond from the heart. Deuteronomy says, "You shall love the Lord your God with all your *heart*" (Dt 6:5; emphasis added). For from the heart come our decisions, our desires, our longings. The heart is called to beat to God's drum.

Yet, there is more, for it is the heart, rather than
the brain, that is the rational center of our lives:

> Let the words of my mouth and
> the meditation of my heart
> be acceptable to you,
> O Lord, my rock and my redeemer. (Ps 19:14)

The *meditation* of my heart! What is this about?
Clearly we attribute thoughts and meditations to
the brain. Just as clearly, the scriptures do not. A
recent article lists the very first scriptural attribute
of the heart as "the source of thought and reason."[2]

The heart can also be a heart of stone. It can be
dead. The prophet Ezekiel laments the hardened
hearts of his people, but he hears God say: "A new
heart I will give you, and a new spirit I will put
within you; and I will remove from your body the
heart of stone and give you a heart of flesh" (Ez
36:26).

Even if not dead, the heart can be deeply hidden, profoundly obscured. The heart can be mysterious. We don't even know our innermost thoughts,
desires, and emotions. We know how to split the
atom, kill millions in one fell swoop, walk on the
moon, connect instantly with others around the
globe—yet we don't know our own hearts. At the
culmination of Psalm 139, the psalmist sings:

> Search me, O God, and know my heart;
> test me and know my thoughts.
> See if there is any wicked way in me,
> and lead me in the way everlasting. (Ps 139:23–24)

The cave of our heart, the center of our being, is often lost to us. In self-defense, we have set up layers and layers to enwrap our hearts. Sometimes it is self-protection: our hearts can be so very vulnerable; our hearts can be made of such very frail flesh. Sometimes it is defilement: our hearts can be so very devious; our hearts can be so very stony. Our hearts can be astray (see Ps 95:10). Sometimes it can be both defense and defilement, all enmeshed together.

Yet, there are differences in these models, and these differences reveal much of the cultures from which the images spring. The self can be all too easily divorced from its context, removed from relationship, understood in isolated splendor. The heart, however, is seen principally in relationship: with others and yet primarily with God. God speaks; the heart listens and responds. "To find the heart is the only means of finding God."[3] Though, I wonder if we don't need so much to find our heart (this has become a task of postbiblical spirituality) as to listen to God's Word and allow it to change our hearts.

Above all else, however, the heart sings to us of embodiment. True, it is a symbol, an image. Yet, it is an embodied symbol—an incarnated image. Our thoughts, our emotions, our desires, our decisions, as seen through the prism of the heart, are all inescapably connected with our bodies. In our disincarnate, cerebral world, how restorative and grounding this is! The colors of autumn are inescapably intertwined with the dwindling daylight.

In like manner, the heart is unthinkable without the body to which it gives life.

These brilliant colors, inevitable harbinger of cooler days and longer nights, summon yet another scriptural image. Fittingly, this illustration is taken straight from creation, a vision of the overarching design of God's intent. "So God created humankind in his image, in the image of God he created them; male and female he created them" (Gn 1:27). At the beginning of Genesis this theme is already present, and in Wisdom, perhaps the last Old Testament book to be written, we also find it. God "made us in the image of his own eternity" (Wis 2:23).

What is this image? Where do we find it in ourselves? It is not in any particular this or that, but rather in the I-don't-know-what that makes us uniquely human. This image is found not only in the head or the heart, the soul or spirit—not only in our bodies either, though they are certainly included—rather, it is found in the totality of us.

We are made in the image of God? We are persons, created by the "three-personed God." Presence, will, desire, consciousness, play, and most of all, freedom—all of these are embodied and incarnated in the physical creation that is the stage for our doing and being. Of such is our personhood. Does this define us? Not hardly! Definition can only be attempted by the objective outsider, and we are certainly not that. We circle around our own essence, perpetually attempting description and perpetually failing.

Our image has moreover lost its luster. It is obscured, downed, and defiled; it is lost deep within the layers of fallenness we find ourselves in. And so our descriptions are at best attempts to describe secondhand; we know only by hearsay the beauty of our creation.

This obscured image of God in us is merely one side of a twofold vision. The other half is found only by prophetic revelation, and by our dim, unquenchable longing for something more. Our desire is not fulfilled with our current reality; we long to grow into the very likeness of God. Here, too, the leaves' transient glory provides a glowing symbol of the fullness and brilliance of our call. We live from the image partially, obscurely; we are called into the transfigured radiance. "Now we see as in a mirror, dimly, but then we will see face to face" (1 Cor 13:12). The splendor of autumn's leaves and grasses reproduces in diminished form the incandescent luminescence of the fullness of life.

What will we be like when we have grown into this radiant likeness? We shall be like the prototype, the second and greater Adam, the one who truly is "the image of the invisible God, the firstborn of all creation" (Col 1:15). Christ is the real Image whom we are called to reproduce.

According to St. Irenaeus of Lyons, "In times past it was said that man was made in God's image, but this was not made evident. For the Word, after whose image man was made, was still unseen. And this was why he so easily lost the likeness. But when the Word of God was made flesh he established both the one and the other: he displayed the true image by himself becoming what his image

was; and he made the likeness secure by uniting
manhood to the likeness of the unseen Father by
means of the visible Word."[4]

Creation itself awaits our return to the true
Image. Humanity is the cosmic hinge upon which
the created world turns. "For the creation waits
with eager longing for the revealing of the children
of God; for the creation was subjected to futility,
not of its own will but by the will of the one who
subjected it, in hope that the creation itself will be
set free from its bondage to decay and will obtain
the freedom of the glory of the children of God"
(Rom 8:19–21).

The glorious leaves will soon be falling, ripped
from the trees by this brisk northwest wind. Decay
soon awaits. The cyclic return of leaves and seasons
and years teaches something beyond decay, something greater and larger. Expand your vision, it
says, look to your true colors. Beyond the seasons,
beyond the years, beyond decay, we are headed for
the glory of God.

bare
november

November is here: cold, gray, empty November. Bare November, with its trees stripped of leaves, with its browns and grays and tans. Dull November. It is a least favorite month for many people.

October's flaming, flamboyant palette of red and orange and gold and yellow and bronze is a tough act to follow, at least here in Maine. Poor, insipid, dull, boring November is squeezed in between the highlights of October and the festivities of December.

True, December is the beginning of winter and can also be bare and cold, with bitter winds and icy rain. But it also brings Advent, that hopeful, joyous prelude to Christmas. Despite being the beginning of the long Maine winter, December is overlaid with the anticipation and joy of the Incarnation.

But the only claim to fame here in central Maine
for poor, desolate November is that it is hunting
season. For those of us who aren't hunters, this
means it is "keep out of the woods" time.

Today is a typical November day: gray, chilly,
moist. It's not cold and raw, however, so in spite
of the possibility of hunters, I take to the woods
appropriately covered in blaze orange. We are
blessed to have our prayer trail: it makes walking
so easy. There is nothing better than a solitary walk
in the woods! This prayer trail is just an old tote
road, once used for bringing out logs. Now bush
hogged once a year for easy walking, it has become
our favorite place for a contemplative stroll.

I take my rosary, so useful for praying the Jesus
Prayer, and I go. My mind is still preoccupied with
the many responsibilities and details of daily life.
I begin repeating, *Lord Jesus Christ, Son of God, have
mercy on us.* Another part of my mind is noticing
the muted colors of the woods, the heavy sky, and
the soft leaves underfoot. It's moist and chilly; the
grass is still green, but with that particular yellowish green that only happens in late fall. There are
fallen leaves everywhere, and they are wet and
soft, not dry and crumbly. Their yellow and red is
mostly gone, faded into tan and brown and a sort
of nondescript mud color. They are on their way to
becoming next year's humus—fodder for another
year's growth.

As I walk down the first hill through the overgrown blueberry fields, I notice there are still some
brilliant red leaves on the wild blueberries. A few
faded, reddish-bronze leaves are on the brambles,

too, and one shrubby young birch still clings to a few golden flags. In the midst of a cluster of trees, a young beech's leaves are fine and full, though now a clear tan. The dry beech leaves often remain on the tree all winter, as do those of the scarlet oaks. *Lord Jesus Christ, Son of God, have mercy on us.*

The taller stalks of grass have gone tan and dry; the milkweed pods are full and dark and have begun bursting open, releasing their cargo of downy, white fluff. Each piece of fluff carries a tiny seed, an embryo of next year's milkweed. This was once a major blueberry-production area. Now all that is left is a small field, which we are struggling to return to production. Only a small field, it still holds several trees and shrubs with a few struggling blueberry vines at their feet. My mind slows, relaxes, the troubles of the day left behind up the hill.

Into the woods now, I see the trees rise bare around me on all sides: gray and black and muted tan. There are oak, birch, maple, beech, and always the ubiquitous poplar—"popple" it is called here in Maine. Young white pines are here also. Underneath are blueberries, brambles, and, rambling everywhere, wintergreen, known locally as checkerberry, its leaves still dark green and glossy. As I round the first bend in the trail, a stone wall appears on my left, a boundary of some long-forgotten field. It approximately marks the middle of what was once a large property. We now own a portion of what had been a larger farm. In the far distance, through the trees, I see the orange flag of a surveyor's ribbon, marking our north boundary.

Ahead on either side is some low terrain. It holds water in spring—and some right now as well. The leaves underfoot are amazing: mostly tan and brown, but the maple leaves that have fallen with their undersides up have turned a dusky shade of muddy blue-gray.

Lord Jesus Christ, Son of God, have mercy on us. My walk continues, and so does the rhythm of my prayer. My mind is now blessedly idle, empty like the month and the day. It is my quiet day, with time for extra prayer, so it's easier to let go of all the tasks to be accomplished, the responsibilities at hand. The movement of my steps matches the prayer. Anger is lulled, anxieties abated. For the moment, both future and past release their hold on me. What is present is the day, the cadence of my steps, the bare trees, the fallen leaves, the feel of the beads sliding through my fingers.

I round the first bend and walk the uneven plateau the land makes before it falls deeply into a second descent. The trail weaves and turns, skirting the up and down of the land. A cluster of lovely white birches appears on my left. I pass them, and tiny, young balsam fir appear on the right, mixed with slightly older pine. And everywhere there is poplar, the quick-growing tree that springs up pervasively in young woods.

Now the trail has bent back southward, and I am approaching the stone wall that marks our south boundary. Here the path turns again, at the top of a steep hill, and takes a long, straight movement to the north, across the land, finding the easiest way down the hill. I pause a short way down. I have reached the end of what was once old blueberry fields. Now I enter older and different woods. There is more pine, mixed with other conifers: hemlock, spruce, fir. Farther down the trail levels out again as it reaches the wetlands. Down below is the place of thick conifers, giant boulders, huge ferns, brambles, and beavers. Near the brook one winter I saw moose tracks and fresh moose droppings. Pausing here, I listen for the "dee-dee-dee" of chickadees and remember that, for some reason, I can always hear them right at this spot, even in the dead of winter.

Lord Jesus Christ, Son of God, have mercy on us. Down below I can see the clearing that was once where wood was yarded out. In the summer it is overgrown with grasses and wildflowers. This, also, is bush hogged and, from a few hundred feet away, it looks like a lovely meadow—a spiritual meadow, I think. Perhaps we should call it that, after the *Spiritual Meadow* of John Moschus. It, too, is showing its November colors: pale green, gold, and tan.

And now I begin the return, which is mostly uphill. I unzip my jacket, aware of how out of shape I am. *Lord Jesus Christ, Son of God, have mercy on us.* I think of my writing, wondering what will emerge next. And quietly something does emerge, simply and smoothly. I think of how wonderful it is to be silent, to have a peaceful mind and heart. Such gift: to be here, alone in the woods, simply receiving the gift of bare trees, daylight, and fallen leaves. Simply receiving. Perhaps that is the gift itself. Even in a cloister, life can become so filled with doing,

with striving, with working. It can be so filled with
things to remember, so filled with responsibilities
and obligations. Today I am reminded of the importance of receiving. The land, the trees, and the fallen
leaves all wait in silence for the approach of winter.
They wait to receive the snow, and they love me
into being with the purity of their emptiness.

The silent woods, this silent walk, has granted
me the empty space in which to receive what God
has to give. Silence—how very precious it is and
how rare. I remember that St. Benedict has an entire
chapter on silence in his *Rule*. He calls it "restraint
of speech."[1] Silence, stillness, and restraint of
speech are uncommon gifts in our noisy and clut-
tered world. Like the bare November woods that
create and embrace an inviting emptiness, they
hold open the space in which to receive God.

Yet, how strange, I reflect, how paradoxical,
that it is two simple yet focused *active* practices
that bring me to this relaxed, contemplative openness, this receptivity, this delicious emptiness.
One of them, walking, is for the body. The other,
a repetitive, seemingly almost mindless formula
of words—though very particular and precious
words, the Jesus Prayer—is for the mind. Together
they have quieted my heart and opened it up to
God. How very striking that activity should so
quickly lead to receptivity, to openness, to the out-
pouring of the Spirit in heart and mind. Yet, this is
precisely what the earliest monastics would also
have said: the active life leads to contemplation.
Like the waxing and waning of the moon, activity

and receptivity are the recurring poles of our journey, weaving in and out of the dance of life.

Activity, like all the energetic growth and
blooming and fruiting of spring and summer in
the natural world, has led to letting go, to bareness,
to emptiness, to receptivity. Receptivity leads to
the Spirit, which in turn engenders life. Life leads
to expression, even to self-expression. "The word
was made flesh." Out of eternal silence, the self-expression of God came into being as word, even as
incarnate Word. And this self-expressive word is
forever engendering new life. The annual cycle of
nature completes itself and recapitulates that of
the spirit.

Lord Jesus Christ, Son of God, have mercy on us.
The prayer continues, as do my steps. I am unaware
of thinking about the future, unaware of plans. Yet,
again—quietly, surely, simply—up wells a thought.
It is only a hint, the beginning of a movement, yet
it is a direction, the next step. Walking and praying
have slowed me down and opened me up. The bare
trees, the empty spaces, have showered me with
this gift. Bare November is the time and space for
receptivity. November may be bare, but it is not
barren.

on the daily manual labor

My knees and shoulders ache as I hurriedly uproot the geraniums from their summer homes in the tubs that grace our entry. Plopping them into pots, I stuff soil around their roots. It's November, and our first real cold is roaring down out of Canada tonight. This is not a touch of frost; this is the full blast, and it's here on our doorstep. I can't linger to cosset the plants along, because I have a long list of tasks to do before the Arctic Express arrives. The parsley needs potting up, and thyme needs transplanting. The Swiss chard needs a double layer of floating row cover to make it through tonight's cold, and I've not yet mulched the recently planted garlic with a deep layer of straw. And the perennial borders! I haven't even begun to cut back the frost-killed tops.

Chapter 48 of St. Benedict's *Rule* is called "On the Daily Manual Labor." He begins it with the stern admonition that "idleness is the enemy of the soul," but I sometimes wonder if he might modify his opinion if he was alive today. In his day, this aphorism was taken seriously by those engaged in following Jesus. Evil was always threatening to descend upon the earnest disciple, and work helped stave it off. Benedict treated work a bit less seriously, realizing that it was to be undertaken out of need, rather than as a desperate stopgap against the inroads of evil. He actually overturned the normal negative attitude to manual labor by requiring *all* the monks to work at it. At the time of the *Rule*, manual labor was slaves' work. Monks worked to fend off the devil; slaves worked out of necessity. Not so for Benedict. Work is redemptive, but work must be done only in measure and as needed, not crammed into every moment of the day. He legislated for about four to six hours of manual labor daily, varying the amount according to the season of the year—varying also according to what needed to be done.

I sometimes wonder if we've come full circle to that pre-Benedictine approach to work, because even in the monastery, work seems to overtake us at every turn, insidiously seeping into all the hours and minutes, like a flood creeping up over our thresholds and threatening to drown us.

Not that we work in order to keep the powers of evil at bay today, unless we think of evil in purely material terms. In solidarity with millions of others, we struggle to pay our bills and to keep our heads above the encroaching waters of poverty and need. But sometimes I wonder if it is all really necessary, if it is really about need. It is so easy to succumb to the powers of advertising, to think we need more and more; and, of course, then we must work to pay for it all. For us at the hermitage, it isn't so much about buying more or having more; it's about maintaining our way of life with only a tiny community. It's about keeping everything looking and performing well. It's about maintaining the buildings, the grounds and gardens, the library, the bakery, the newsletter and communications. It's about providing hospitality and retreat for those who come to the retreat house, and ensuring they have good meals and a clean and inviting place for their time here. It's about being present to people when they need an ear to listen, a heart to hear their pains and difficulties or to share in their joys. Most of all, it is about maintaining and even improving our prayer in community, the Office—and our personal prayer as well.

As October moves into November, and November begins its inexorable descent into winter, another task looms over our heads. Advent is approaching, and with Advent comes *fruitcake season!* For those who don't know us, fruitcake season is our in-house name for the four to six weeks leading up to Christmas. Throughout the year, at a leisurely pace, we bake fruitcakes. It's a labor-intensive process. First the fruit and nuts are soaked in brandy for forty-eight hours. Then the cakes are baked. Once cooled, they are wrapped in brandy-soaked cloths, placed in airtight containers, and stacked in our fruitcake cellar, which is designed to keep them cool and moist throughout the year. For at least six months they sit in the cool, humid darkness, gracefully aging, their brandy flavor mellowing.

Suddenly fruitcake season is upon us. One by one the containers are hauled out. One by one the cakes are unwrapped. One by one they are splashed with more brandy, then decorated with cherries and nuts. One by one they are wrapped in plastic and gift-boxed. One by one—or sometimes by two or four or six or even eight—they are packed in shipping boxes and sent out.

This, unfortunately, is not a leisurely process—anything but! Hundreds of cakes are baked over the course of the year and put to sleep in the chill darkness of the fruitcake cellar. Those same hundreds are hurriedly unwrapped, decorated, and shipped—all in the space of a very few weeks. The process is time consuming, labor intensive, and exhausting.

It also happens at the end of the year—just at the time when the busy garden season is winding down, and the equally busy retreat season is still in high gear. I enter fruitcake season already tired and especially tired of work. But there it is, staring me in the face: fruitcake season—a necessary evil, for it's our major source of income.

Fruitcake season arrives here in Maine at the very time when all the leaves are off the trees and the ground is bare and silently waiting for the coming of winter and its covering of snow. The earth stands revealed in all its hills and hollows. The bare simplicity of the land entices me to walk and look and simply be present to its quiet restfulness, stillness, and peace.

How often, in this season of waiting and watching, I long to let myself be drawn into the stillness. Yet, with Robert Frost, I, too, know that I have "miles to go before I sleep." Miles of packing and shipping. Miles of work getting our almost-but-not-quite finished new addition ready to be lived in. Miles of cleaning and helping in the bakery. Miles and miles of phone calls and notes to write. Miles of trying to be very present to people who come on retreat or for spiritual direction, or who just come for a fruitcake or cookies and who might need a listening ear.

Fruitcake season, the busiest work season of our year, comes during Advent. I often think that Advent is about watching and waiting—with the earth, the moon, and the stars—for the coming of the Lord in the form of a tiny infant, at the darkest hour, in Bethlehem. It is a time of trying to be still, a time of trying to listen very deeply for the voice of the Lord.

Paradoxically, for us and for so many, it is often the busiest time of the year. The pre-Christmas rush of shopping and cooking and remembering others and getting together with friends and family often pulls us away from our attempts to be quiet and to listen to God's voice. We are caught, it seems—in spite of our best intentions—in between the times of quiet and the noisy, messy rush of getting everything ready. We are caught in the middle, pulled in two directions, and find ourselves precariously balancing between this busy, hurried, boisterous daily time and the still, peaceful, quiet yet powerful attraction of eternal time, other time, ageless time.

There is *always* the daily manual labor. Benedict surely knew this. There are *always* lots of other things in life as well. Benedict knew this just as surely, for his chapter is also about lectio, the daily spiritual reading, and prayer, and the times for meals. Manual labor must be done, but so must everything else. We labor at many things: our prayer, our lectio, our relationships. The difficulty is in keeping them balanced, and Benedict wisely regulates the balance: so much time for manual labor, so much time for prayer, so much time for each element of the day. It is a worthy ideal, one for which we always strive—especially today, when work seems to be a ravening lion, threatening to gobble up everything else we do. The fruitcake-season lion is necessary, providing for many of our material needs, yet it, too, gobbles relentlessly at our leisure time, our prayer time, our community time. How then can we be attentive to the quiet, loving voice of the Lord, heard so delicately in silence? How can we even hear our own voices, or those of each other, in such a time of work and pressure?

One thing this coming feast of the Incarnation tells us, loud and clear, is that there is no time, no person, no circumstance, that is removed from God's blessed influence. The Lord came in the flesh, and so how can our flesh, however beset, be absent from God's loving care?

We are tugged and pulled in so many various ways and often overworked, and even in the midst of this, the Lord is hidden "in spirit and in power," as St. Bernard says. God comes to us "in between," hidden in the heart of the busyness and the rush and the multitasking. At the same time God draws our hearts to the quiet and the peace and the stillness, asking us to come apart and rest awhile. As long as we live in this life, we await his coming in fullness in our lives—and we struggle to balance the competing demands of work, prayer, play, and rest—even as St. Benedict did.

We live always in perpetual Advent, and at the same time in perpetual fruitcake season, awaiting the fullness of revelation, truth, and grace. Yet, we share the consolation of knowing God has already come for us, in the form of an infant who grew to adulthood, and shared all the in-between times and spaces—including work—of a human life.

There will always be the daily manual labor. Often there will be days and even weeks when there is too much work, seasons that are out of balance. I remind myself that fruitcake season will soon be over. What awaits is winter, when there is no baking, no rush, no packages to mail. Soon we will enter into our long quiet season. We may need to think of this as the season of manual labor, which is then balanced by the season of quiet. Each of us, whether in or out of a monastery, must find our own way to balance our work with all the other elements of our existence.

In this life we will always juggle the competing demands of work, prayer, rest, and play, reminding ourselves of the Lord who also was overwhelmed by his work and sought to get away for quiet times of prayer and rest. We remember also that the Lord is with us in all these challenging and competing needs. Here we are pilgrims on the way, but even in the midst of all our work and cares, we await the time when the daily manual labor will have ended and we are at rest forever.

stillness

For years, even decades, I have fruitlessly fought against winter. Shortly before moving to Maine I had nightmares in which I was driving north, and the farther north I drove, the deeper and higher were the banks of snow along the highway. During my first years in Maine, I kept looking for somewhere else to go, some other place to live. Finally, after six long years, I quit fighting and accepted that this is where God had called me to be. But I still didn't like winter.

My favorite season was always late summer, when the bugs were finally gone, and everything was in full flower and fruit. The garden would be overflowing with lovely veggies and fruits, the flowers would be those of late summer and early autumn, the butterflies and bees would be making the rounds from flower to flower, the work of the garden would be mostly done, and I could enjoy the harvest.

Lately I've realized more precisely what is so difficult for me about winter. It's the absence of earth. If my feet don't connect with bare earth, I feel somehow rootless, ungrounded. It's an unsettling and disturbing feeling. Plus I feel trapped by the snow: stuck inside a warm building, only able to walk on cleared driveways or paths. I can't wander around to check out how the trees and shrubs are doing, can't trot down the prayer trail to let the quiet of the empty woods sink reverently into my soul. A few years ago I discovered snowshoeing, which was a wonderful help, but since then a series of slight injuries—to a knee, to a hip, to a foot— have conspired to keep me off snowshoes. So once again I have the sense of being trapped, a prisoner of snow and ice.

These last few months a new awareness emerged. High summer isn't my favorite season anymore. Underneath the surface of consciousness, without my even noticing, something has changed. Now what I love is the bare ground and empty trees of November. I drink in the emptiness. I love the fading yellowish green of the grass, the browns and blacks and grays of the tree trunks, the spaces between them that lead the eye down and down and down into the far distance. I love the bare stillness of it all. The earth stands revealed in all its simple beauty, undisguised by leaves and grasses and shrubs. The curve of a meadow, the height of a hill, the swoop of a steep downhill slope—these are balm to my soul, sated as it is with the tasks and the variety and the clutter of spring and summer with all their many responsibilities and desires.

Just the other day I had an amazing new insight. Winter brings quiet. Winter brings stillness. Winter brings relief from the work of baking and shipping and dealing with people. Winter brings rest. Snow guards the cloister, keeping others away and ourselves within, unable to do even the most important of errands. A revelation! Perhaps, after all these years, I may learn to appreciate winter.

Stillness is something I have admired and desired for even more decades than I've feared winter. I often think I am a natural born *apophatic*—someone who loves the path of darkness, of bareness, of going beyond the positive ways of finding God to the *via negativa*. God is greater than all that is, and so is found in the stillness that is beyond feelings, beyond words, beyond concepts or images or thoughts. Stillness is a contemplative posture, a waiting for God's Word to be quietly received in the stillness of heart and mind and soul. It is symbolized by Mary, receiving the Word into her faith and heart and even her flesh: "Let it be with me according to your word" (Lk 1:38). Stillness has a long and deeply respected history in contemplative life, especially among hermits and with the Orthodox East: stillness, or *hesychia;* or rest, *quies;* receptivity.

In the Christian East, *hesychia* is the name for the contemplative life, the life of stillness. Those who live it are called hesychasts. The tradition springs from that flowering of the undivided Church in the fourth century, the Desert Fathers and Mothers. It had another flowering among the twelfth-century Orthodox monks on Mt. Athos, and has continued as a living, vital tradition among Orthodox to this day. Hesychasts attempt to live a life of stillness. To do so, they often live as individual hermits or in small groups of hermits, far removed from the noise, commotion, and disruption of the world. They practice silence and manual labor, and they dedicate themselves to following the Lord Jesus in all virtue. They also often practice the Jesus Prayer.

Today the snow is falling thickly, its whiteness backgrounded by the gray of the forest. When it snows, there is a marvelous physical stillness. All sound is hushed by these intricate, tiny, swirling, dancing white flakes.

The snow enforces physical stillness. Inner stillness arrives by sheer gift. There are times when God's hand hovers over us, and all our inner noise is hushed. We are dropped into a place beyond words, below thoughts, far from emotion and desire. All is stilled, and we are in Presence. If words arise, they are simple, profound, grateful. Tears may flow in this blessed, peace-filled spaciousness.

Such times are beyond our striving or control or even imagining. They simply are—and they are God's gift. Our lives, for a moment, are filled with the peace beyond all understanding, with the love that called us into being. We are fulfilled, enriched, in stillness—hesychia.

We can never make this stillness happen. Nor can we sustain it voluntarily. For we have an enemy within our very mind—our own thoughts, tugging us this way and that, and all too often in the direction of our own obsessions and compulsions. Yet, though stillness always remains a gift, there is a way to prepare for it, a way to work toward it. We can use everything in our lives to point us in this direction if throughout the days and months and years we continually strive to bring all the contradictions and convolutions of our lives into integration. The early desert tradition has a name for this goal. It was called purity of heart, and it was seen as the proximate goal, the final yet most necessary and important step in entering into the kingdom of heaven.

How do we achieve purity of heart? These early Christians understood that the path led through the traditional disciplines of asceticism.

Practices such as fasting, meditation, prayer, solitude, silence, and vigils help retrain and refocus human energies and desires and redirect them in orderly fashion toward God. In particular, the asceticism of fasting, vigils, and—for monastics—celibacy, disciplines bodily energies and reorients them to God. The practice of active virtues—feeding the hungry, tending the sick, visiting prisoners, relieving distress of any kind—all help reorder fractured social disharmonies. It also enables the aspiring ascetic to move her attention away from herself and toward others and their needs and aspirations.

There is an inner asceticism also, in which we strive to be attentive to our thoughts, especially those that are negative. Following our thoughts helps us to understand and transform them, by replacing them with the meditative repetition of sacred phrases and words. We can take a word or phrase from our daily lectio to repeat throughout the day, to help us when we are attracted by

negative thoughts of any kind. Or, like the hesychasts of Mt. Athos and the eighteenth-century
Russian pilgrim, we, too, can practice the Jesus
Prayer. Echoing the Gospel prayer of the publican,
focusing on this prayer is seen as the most powerful means of calling our often scattered and distracted minds and hearts into recollection. Indeed it
is believed to be the most powerful prayer possible,
for in praying it, we call directly upon the all-pow-
erful name of Jesus.

The hesychasts, those ardent devotees of stillness, might disparage much of contemporary psychology, which many today believe to be a cure
for all ills. Rather, they have their own forms of
psychology, based on the ancient understanding
of the human person found in the scriptures and
developed by the early Desert Abbas and Ammas.
At best they would see Western psychology as a
sometimes necessary prelude to the real work of
bringing together our minds and hearts and cen-
tering them on Jesus. In this holy work, they might
say, the Jesus Prayer is the finest tool, an unsur-
passed asceticism that turns us away from all else
and unites us to God.

Lately, stillness eludes me. The Jesus Prayer is a
matter of rote. Even the scriptures seem dull. What
causes this? I do not know. Does winter still affect
me? Is it a residue of fatigue after a very busy and
tiring year, filled with work and responsibilities?
It is the remnants of a head cold that lingered way
beyond its time? Or is it something deeper, an inner
resistance? Could it be *acedia*, the noonday devil,
that listlessness and boredom that affects all of us

at times, and that figures so largely in the pantheon of demons inventoried by those Desert Abbas?

What would I do, I wonder, if I were to treat myself as someone looking for spiritual accompaniment? I would ask questions, lots of questions. And so I do. I hear myself asking what else has been going on in my life, and I hear the answers: busyness, responsibility, the construction, the baking and shipping, the fatigue, the head cold, the desire for time and rest and space. I nod—that is normal; that is unsurprising. We all need time to recuperate after prolonged periods of challenging activity and responsibility, and also after sickness.

But what else is happening here? I ask myself. This resistance to the Jesus Prayer is of longer duration. There seem to be two aspects to the difficulty. Often, when there is nothing else to mandate my immediate attention, I remain unwilling to attend to this prayer, preferring instead to let my mind wander at will. Further, it is difficult for me to say the words of this prayer, even interiorly, mentally. I long instead for silence and stillness. Even these very powerful and precious words are too limited, too effortful, too verbose.

I ponder this powerful and long-lasting resistance. I remind myself that where there is great resistance, there is the potential for great life. In some ways, this resistance seems good, as in my reluctance to engage in wordiness, even the limited and gracious words of the Jesus Prayer. Yet, my unwillingness to focus on the prayer during times of unfocused attention is potentially more negative.

What is this about? Can this unwillingness be laziness? Or is it actually a right response?

What exactly am I resisting? Why am I so unwilling to concentrate on the prayer? Why do I prefer my own thoughts so much? And what thoughts are they, anyway? Perhaps that is a helpful question and a way to delineate the difficulty.

Sometimes, the thoughts are negative: thoughts of anger, or worries and anxieties. At other times, they are more idle and free-floating, almost a daydream, an escape. The negative thoughts feel like a heavy burden, a prison, something I am trapped in. But the others can be delightful, not necessarily in their content, but in the sense of relaxation and release they bring. Daydreaming, fantasy, imagination—all of this is conducive to play and to receptivity, and receptivity can open us to the Spirit. I've noticed that this often happens while driving, at least on relatively untraveled roads. At those times I love to observe what is passing: sunlight on the trees, a hawk circling in a cerulean sky, freshly mown hay, or a stream tumbling its way downhill over scattered rocks—the lovely variety of creation in all its moods. I note also what is happening in the human sphere: fresh paint on an old building, the details on a church steeple, old junked cars sitting sadly in a yard with weeds growing through their windows—the ordinary manifestations of human achievement and human neglect. "Never let go of a holy curiosity," Einstein once said, and I realize that this is a holy curiosity. More, it is a receptivity to the variety, beauty, and infinite otherness of God's creation.

Aha! At last I know when it is important to focus, and when not. This ancient practice of "following the thoughts" has proved itself once again. When the thoughts are negative, obsessive, or anxious, then it is the time to focus, to practice the prayer, to move my attention away from the thoughts and toward God's loving mercy. When the thoughts are innocent, playful, and imaginative, they leave me open and receptive. This in itself is a movement toward God. To bring my focus back to the words of any prayer, however wonderful, would pull me away from the leading of the Spirit. I marvel at the delicacy of the inner movements of God's Spirit at work in conjunction with my spirit, a human spirit. How attentive I must be at each moment to the Spirit's presence in my life.

Today the snow is falling again, but not silently. Today a blizzard roars outside my window. The snow falls so heavily that I can't even see the blueberry field, a mere fifty feet away. A five-foot drift blocks the cloister door. Today the storm is outside. But inside, there is stillness. God's Spirit hovers over me, and stillness blossoms forth in the midst of my heart and mind. What a blessed gift is stillness, hesychia, *quies*. What a blessed gift of the Spirit. What a creative fruition of heart and mind. All the fullness of human and divine love and creativity is here enclosed in this seemingly insignificant gift of obscure and wordless peace. Here, in this blessed stillness, nothing happens—nothing except the gift of God's love.

epilogue:
memories

"Hodie Christus natus est; hodie salvator apparuit." The haunting, ancient chant arises from the enveloping darkness. The soft radiance of candles creates globes of gentle light at the margins of sight. The tiny church, nearly two centuries old, with its wooden floors, brick walls, and old, hard pews, creates the perfect acoustic space for the a cappella choir's Advent performance. "Today Christ is born; today salvation has appeared." They begin and end their performance with this ancient monastic chant, processing in and out with it—much as did monastics throughout the centuries, as they entered their churches for Vigils of Christmas Day.

This is an annual performance by a local, but nationally renowned, high school choir. We can't always attend, but this year we came because one of the singers is the son of a friend of ours. He's now a senior. We haven't seen him in years, and we're amazed to find he's well over six feet tall, and blessed with a wonderful bass voice.

This particular choir comes from the town in which our hermitage was formerly located, so meeting our friends and their son after a gap of nearly six years is a particular pleasure. Before the performance we are busy catching up on news and events, and also busily greeting many current friends from the parish. All the while my eye is repeatedly caught by a woman sitting in the pew behind. She looks familiar, yet I can't quite place her. She leans forward, says my name, and smiles. I say hello but am obviously uncertain. "I'm Tommy's mom," she says.

"Tommy's mom!" Tommy was the teenager who many years ago helped mow our lawns and shovel our paths. He shoveled off the roof a few times, too, when there was way too much snow. Tommy was a great worker, a fine young man, and so reliable, too. I mention this to Carleen, his mom. "How amazing!" she said. "He'd never work for me."

"That's because you're Mom," I replied. We both laugh, knowing it's true.

Then we're away, cresting the wave of, "Do you remember?" and "How is so-and-so?"

"What's happened to Harriet?" she asks. "I want to Google her, and I'm so afraid I'll pull up her obituary."

"You won't believe it," I reply. "I just heard from her and her daughter. They sent a photo of Harriet on her 103rd birthday!"

"103!" she exclaims. "That's incredible!"

"I'll send you the picture," I say.

~eeee~

The choir enters in darkness, carrying candles, and encircles the congregation with their compelling and extremely moving chant. "*Hodie Christus natus est.*" Today Christ is born. Today salvation appears. Today!

Time folds its wings, envelops me, condenses, and dissolves. Today, and tomorrow, and yesterday are all suddenly and immediately present. I am enveloped in luminous memories of our days in Thorndike: the hermitage there, the land, the gardens, and the friends. I am surrounded by friends past and present, all enclosed in this welcoming space and this soaring, glorious sound.

I remember the hermitage, simple and inviting, with white walls and wood ceiling. I remember the evenings, when it seemed as though the space within it was alive with Presence. I remember the deck, with its wonderful view, and sunsets over the distant mountains. I remember the gardens, the hot summer days, and the stillness of early Sunday mornings. I remember sunflowers, and picking sugar snap peas, which Katy, Sr. Bernadette's black dog, loved to beg for.

Our tiny chapel emerges into my interior gaze, with its Sunday afternoons of adoration. I remember also Wednesday mornings and Mass, and the gathering for coffee and cookies afterward.

I remember moving there at the end of August, more than twenty years ago, knowing nobody. I remember a knock on my door a few months later on a cold December evening, and Carleen standing there, introducing herself, and inviting me up for a pre-Christmas supper. Tommy was only seven then, and her youngest child was not even born. Twenty years of memories surround me, as do past friends, and so many wonderful current friends, and this tiny country church where I am now at home. I have been so blessed, so very, very blessed.

Twenty years of memories, of struggle, of growth, of blessings are all present and enfolded in this moment. For twenty years of gift, and this moment now to remember and celebrate, I give thanks.

This moment of epiphany is in my mind in these days after Christmas, as the year winds down. I marvel as I recall that it happened in the midst of the pre-Christmas rush, the busiest time of year for us, when it seems that all we did was decorate fruitcakes, take orders for fruitcakes, and pack and ship fruitcakes. Yet, in the midst of all this, like a flower unfolding its petals, or a firework explosively showering me with droplets of glory, the benediction of memories was given to me.

And yet, in spite of this experience, not all memories are golden. Not all are loving and wonderful. We each have moments of blessing and gift, but also moments—sometimes days, weeks, even years—of sadness, suffering, and pain. As this year draws to a close, I remember also the difficulties of our former home: the brutal winters, with the winds whipping down from the faraway mountains. The wind-driven snow made a mockery of our attempts to keep open the paths to our chapel and remain faithful to our hours of prayer there. I remember a few not-so-friendly neighbors and townspeople. I remember apathy and those who derided our life of prayer—not to mention all the long hours of work to build up the hermitage, and the struggles to learn to grow together as a community of solitaries. Many very difficult memories also flood through my mind. Life can be challenging at best, and at worst overwhelmingly filled with sadness and suffering

What of memories such as these? These are not golden. These did not come to my mind in a radiant moment of epiphany. Yet, they are still there.

Do such moments not count somehow in the eternal scheme of things, I wonder? Or do I perhaps dissociate and just let them drop out of sight? How do we juxtapose such wonder and presence with the wholeness of life, which is not only good, but bad as well—joyous yet often conflicted and tormented?

Today we are in the beginning of a four-day "snow event," a combination of several storms that will envelop Maine for the next several days and leave us with enormous heaps of snow everywhere. Maine is known for its long and difficult winters. In spite of many lovely winter scenes, I find memories

of storms and their aftereffects to be mostly negative. I remember the famous ice storm of '98, when
it poured freezing rain for several days. Much of
the state was left without power. After the rain
stopped, I would slide out to chip away at the thick
coating of ice on our car. It took hours of work just
to get the door open! During those hours I would
often hear a huge boom and crash as another large
tree came down, snapped off by the weight of the
ice. We were without power or even phone for
more than eleven days. We had friends without
these for sixteen days, and even twenty. These are
remembrances of difficult, challenging, traumatic
days.

How do we reconcile these to all the wonderful memories? How can we blend these disparate
elements into wholeness? Is it even possible? T. S.
Eliot writes,

> Time present and time past
> Are both perhaps present in time future,
> And time future contained in time past.
> If all time is eternally present
> All time is unredeemable.[1]

If all time were to be eternally present to us, it
would indeed be unredeemable, unsupportable,
unendurable. Why then should twenty years of
memory suddenly blossom and merge with present
in glorious fusion?

Eliot may provide the resolution of this
dilemma later in the same poem when he says,
"Time past and time future allow but a little consciousness. To be conscious is not to be in time."

What a strange statement this seems, until we recall that for Eliot, as for any believer, consciousness includes far more than the transitory beat that we call time.

> Only in time can the moment in the rose-garden,
> The moment in the arbour where the rain beat,
> The moment in the draughty church at smokefall
> Be remembered; involved with past and future.
> Only through time time is conquered.[2]

Only through time time is conquered. Duration, memories, twenty years, time past, time present—all open themselves toward the approach of the future, coalescing in a few wondering moments out of time, filled with Presence. Can time exclude the griefs, the sorrows, the struggles, the work, the fears, even the horrors?

"When the fullness of time had come, God sent his son"—not in eternity, but in time—"born of a woman, born a subject of the law" (Gal 4:4). Flesh and blood like us, he was subject to time, to vicissitude, to memory; to suffering, horror, and death; "that he might redeem those subject to the law" (Gal 4:5). The Word was born into time, made subject to time, that he might redeem all of our times. *Only through time time conquered.* Embracing the Word and following the Word throughout our time enables us to redeem time—not so much to conquer it perhaps, but to transcend it.

"With the Lord one day is like a thousand years" (2 Pt 3:8). But this is not so for us! Even in this moment of epiphany, when time condensed, it was still time, duration, but only condensed into a marvelous overview and filled with depths of meaning and significance. Not for nothing is Christianity a historical religion. The Word entered time and therefore history. In this process time and history took on ultimate consequence. Only through time is time redeemed and transcended.

All of this would be meaningless without memory, which gives time its structure and coherence. In a famous chapter of the *Confessions* devoted to memory, St. Augustine says, "Great is this power of memory, exceeding great, O my God,—an inner chamber large and boundless! Who has plumbed the depths thereof? Yet it is a power of mine, and appertains unto my nature; nor do I myself grasp all that I am. Therefore is the mind too narrow to contain itself."[3] Our memory is a marvel, as Augustine notices. It contains the entire world and even more within it. It is larger than ourselves, and yet it is contained within us. Without it we would have no sense of before and after, no past or future. Perhaps, unendurably, we would have no sense of self.

What then of that vitally important spiritual tradition, which teaches us that we should always strive to live in the present? What about the "sacrament of the present moment," so eloquently spoken of by Jean-Pierre de Caussade? What about Br. Lawrence's practice of the presence of God, in which we are taught to pay attention to this present moment, for it is the place of God's presence?

The present moment is indeed the time and place where we connect with God, the special locus of God's presence. We all tend to live too much in the past (usually by way of regret or wishfulness), or in the future (usually by way of fear or desire). It is indeed this present moment, this *now*, in which we find God's presence and help and salvation. Yet, this present moment cannot conclusively be cut off from past or future. Alzheimer's patients live only in the present, and yet it seems impossible to call that a real and blessed life.

Rather, living in the present and connecting to God in the present must be contextualized by memory of the past—and of God's actions in our past—and also by hope for the future. This dialectic affects our relationship both to past and future, and provides a foundation that is trust. Holding ourselves in God's loving gaze in the present moment, we have the potential to transform both our memories and our future. Memory is gift and blessing, and it is indeed formative for our future, as long as it is not cut off from the present.

Memory is indeed gift and blessing. Even the memories that are particularly difficult for us—those we would very much prefer to forget, like the Holocaust, or even our own personal holocausts—are part of the wholeness of our lives. If we do not remember them, at least to some degree, we cannot redeem them. Only through remembrance are they brought back into time, and redeemed and transformed. Memory is what gives us knowledge of ourselves, both the good and the bad. Knowledge of self gives us knowledge of God, for we are made in God's image, and God resides with us and within us. Our memories of ourselves, in some mysterious way, give us access to God.

Memory is vitally important in yet another way, especially in the early monastic tradition. *Memoria Dei*, the remembrance of God, was understood as the way to connect to God and to remain steadfastly in God's presence. "Let each one of us set on our souls the seal of the divine form and figure by the assiduous recollection and memory of God."[4] Forgetfulness was for them—as for us—a deadly disease, leading us far from ourselves, and therefore from God.

Our moments of memory, such as my epiphany at the concert, may be a very positive experience. They may equally well be negative. Yet, the Word has entered into time, with all its weight of memory, and in doing so has given us the opportunity to transform all memories, both positive and negative. Indeed all memory, even the most despairing, is now packed with meaning and significance for those who believe. The Advent concert happened to be a positive experience of meaning and mystery, a wonderful brief moment out of time yet filled to brimming with moments and recollections of twenty years of time. "A good measure, pressed down, shaken together, running over, will be poured into your lap" (Lk 6:38): the fullness of gift. But what is the meaning of a moment of memory? What does it signify? What a mystery it is! It is a mystery of past and present, of memories and of the here-and-now, and most of all, of Presence.

"Mystery is participated presence because I share from the inside the life of God, who is known and unknowable," says contemporary poet Kilian McDonnell, O.S.B. [5] These memories, this life, these friends, these places, these gardens—all are caught up in something much greater. All are caught up and participate in the life of God. I know this, yet it is too great to know. It is beyond knowing, as God is both "known and unknowable."

At year's end, we remember. Perhaps, like St. Julian of Norwich, we shall be fortunate. She, too, was caught up in something both known and unknowable, a series of visions or "shewings" that came to her as she lay deathly ill. Julian spent the next thirty-three years remembering these and pondering their meaning. Perhaps like her, as we ponder the meaning of our memories and our lives, we will be blessed to say, "All shall be well, and all manner of thing shall be well" in God's remembrance and our own.[6]

notes

Bare Bones

1. Origen, *Contra Celsus* 2.67, quoted in Olivier Clement, *The Roots of Christian Mysticism* (New York: New City Press, 1982), 38.

2. Theophilus of Antioch, "Three Books to Autolycus," quoted in Clement, *Roots of Christian Mysticism*, 73.

Blessed Boredom

1. Benedicta Ward, S.L.G., trans., *The Sayings of the Desert Fathers: The Alphabetical Collection* (London: Mowbray, 1975), 139.

2. Baron Wormser, *The Road Washes Out in Spring: A Poet's Memoir of Living Off the Grid* (Hanover, NH: University Press of New England, 2006), 32.

Qoheleth's Paradox

1. Martin Laird, *A Sunlit Absence* (New York: Oxford University Press, 2011), 72.

2. Ibid., 82.

3. Kathleen M. O'Connor, *The Wisdom Literature*, Message of Biblical Spirituality, no. 5 (Collegeville, MN: Liturgical Press, 1988), 131.

Seeds of Wisdom

1. Benedict, *RB 1980, The Rule of St. Benedict: In Latin and English with Notes*, ed. Timothy Fry, O.S.B. (Collegeville, MN: Liturgical Press, 1981), 20:3, 217.

Gifts of the Spirit

1. Augustine, *The Confessions and Letters of Augustine: With a Sketch of His Life and Work*, in *Nicene and Post-Nicene Fathers:*

First Series, vol. 1, ed. Philip Schaff, D.D., L.L.D. (Peabody, MA: Hendrickson, 1994), 10.1.1.

2. James Carroll, *Practicing Catholic* (New York: Houghton Mifflin Harcourt, 2009), 15.

3. Thomas Merton, *Contemplative Prayer* (Garden City, NY: Image Books, 1971), 88.

Ordinary Time

1. Jean-Pierre de Caussade, *Abandonment to Divine Providence*, trans. John Beevers (New York: Doubleday, 1975), 41.

2. Ibid., 43.

3. Ibid., 51.

4. Jon Kabat-Zinn, *Wherever You Go, There You Are: Mindfulness Meditation in Everyday Life* (New York: Hyperion, 1994), 16.

5. Ibid., 4.

6. Robert Frost, "Not All There," in *The Poetry of Robert Frost: The Collected Poems, complete and unabridged*, ed. Edward Connery Lathem (New York: Holt, Rinehart & Winston, 1979), 309.

7. Bernard of Clairvaux, *The Cistercian World: Monastic Writings of the Twelfth Century*, trans. and ed. Pauline Matarasso (New York: Penguin Books, 1993), 78.

Ah, Roses!

1. John of the Cross, "The Spiritual Canticle," in *The Collected Works of St. John of the Cross* (Washington, DC: ICS Publications, 1973), 112.

Japanese Beetles

1. John Cassian, *The Institutes*, trans. Boniface Ramsey, O.P., Ancient Christian Writers, no. 58 (New York: Newman Press, 2000), 193.

2. Ibid., 203–4.

3. Hesychios, *The Philokalia, vol. I*, compiled by Nikodimos of the Holy Mountain and Makarios of Corinth, trans. and ed. G.F.H. Palmer, Philip Sherrard, and Kallistos Ware (London: Faber and Faber, 1979), 190.

Walking on Water

1. Bruno Barnhart, *The Good Wine: Reading John from the Center* (Mahwah, NJ: Paulist Press, 1993), 65.
2. Ibid., 69.

Good to Be Here

1. Adalbert de Vogue, "The Divine Office" in *The Rule of Saint Benedict* (Kalamazoo, MI: Cistercian Publications, 1983), 141.
2. Ibid., 142.
3. Ibid., 144.
4. Michael Casey, *The Undivided Heart: The Western Monastic Approach to Contemplation* (Petersham, MA: St. Bede's Publications, 1994), 88.
5. De Vogue, *Rule of Saint Benedict*, 153.

Abundance

1. "Scarcity," *Wikipedia*, accessed September 16, 2015, http://en.wikipedia.org/wiki/Scarcity.
2. St. Isaac of Syria Skete, e-mail message to authors, July 29, 2010.

Goldenrod Days

1. "Salve Festa Dies," *A Millennium of Music: The Benedictine Tradition*, ArmorArtis Chamber Choir, Johannes Somary, Conductor (International Order of Benedictines, 2001), liner notes, 60.
2. Cassian, *The Institutes*, 211.
3. In Jordan E. Rosenfeld, "A Woman of Letters: Isabel Allende," *Writer's Digest* 88, no. 5 (2008): 41.

Diminishment

1. Quoted by a student of Adrian Van Kamm in a personal communication with the author.
2. Wendell Berry, *The Unsettling of America: Culture and Agriculture* (San Francisco: Sierra Books, 1977), 95.

Approaching Darkness

1. Gregory of Nyssa, *The Life of Moses*, trans. Abraham J. Malherbie and Everett Ferguson, The Classics of Western Spirituality (New York: Paulist Press, 1978), 82–83.
2. Ibid., 93; emphasis added.
3. Ibid., 95; emphasis added.

True Colors

1. Thomas Merton, quoted in James Finley, *Merton's Palace of Nowhere* (Notre Dame, IN: Ave Maria Press, 1978), 27.
2. Harriet Luckman, *Purity of Heart in Early Ascetic and Monastic Literature: Essays in Honor of Juana Raasch, O.S.B.* (Collegeville, MN: Liturgical Press, 1999), 18.
3. Casey, *Undivided Heart*, 40.
4. Irenaeus of Lyons, quoted in Aelred Squire, *Asking the Fathers* (New York: Paulist Press, 1973), 22.

Bare November

1. Benedict, *RB 1980, The Rule of St. Benedict*, chapter 6.

Epilogue: Memories

1. T. S. Eliot, *Four Quartets*, in *The Complete Poems and Plays 1909–1950* (New York: Harcourt, Brace and World, 1971), 117.
2. Ibid., 119–20.
3. Augustine, *Confessions*, in Schaff, *Nicene and Post Nicene Fathers*, 10.9.15.
4. Basil the Great, *Small Asceticon, Reg 2492b*, quoted in Casey, *Undivided Heart*, 67.
5. Kilian McDonnell, O.S.B., "A Poet in the Monastery: I Do Not 'Tell Noble Lies,'" *The American Benedictine Review* 59 no. 3 (2008): 247.
6. Julian of Norwich, *Showings*, trans. and ed. Edmund Colledge, O.S.A., and James Walsh, S.J., The Classics of Western Spirituality (New York: Paulist Press, 1978), 151.

Sr. Elizabeth Wagner lives a contemplative life of prayer and solitude at Transfiguration Hermitage, a semi-eremitical community she founded that follows the Rule of St. Benedict. Sr. Wagner is a hermit, writer, spiritual director, and retreat leader. She also serves as formation director, gardener, and groundskeeper of the hermitage.

Raised on a farm in Connecticut, Sr. Wagner graduated with a degree in humanities from Shimer College in Illinois. She was attending Andover Newton Theological School when she found her Catholic faith and her love of contemplative prayer. She then entered a Carmelite monastery, but left in search of more solitude. Sr. Wagner also served as adjunct professor of Christian spirituality at Bangor Theological Seminary.

She regularly writes for the quarterly newsletter of the hermitage and has written book reviews and essays for a number of religious and literary publications. Sr. Wagner was awarded *Willow Review*'s 2011 award for nonfiction. She is a member of the American Benedictine Academy, Maine Writers and Publishers Alliance, and the Coastal Maine Botanical Gardens.

She lives in Windsor, Maine.